GROWTH AND EQUALITY IN RURAL CHINA

The Asian Employment Programme is an integral part of the ILO's World Employment Programme. Its main objectives are to identify the factors which prevent a substantial expansion of employment opportunities in countries in the Asian Region, to identify measures which can overcome these factors and to assist governments in the implementation of such measures. The Asian Regional Team for Employment Promotion (ARTEP) based in Bangkok is responsible for implementing the Asian Employment Programme.

GROWTH AND EQUALITY
IN RURAL CHINA

by
Keith Griffin
and
Ashwani Saith

ASIAN EMPLOYMENT PROGRAMME

ISBN 92-2-102422-9 Limp Cover US$10
ISBN 92-2-102427-X Hard Cover US$15

First published 1981

ILO publication can be obtained through major booksellers or ILO local offices in many countries, or direct from ILO Publications, International Labour Office, CH-1211 Geneva 22, Switzerland. A catalogue or list of new publications will be sent free of charge from the above address.

Distributed by
Maruzen Asia Pte. Ltd.,
P.O. Box 67, Pasir Panjang,
Singapore 9111.

Printed by Koon Wah Printing Pte. Ltd., Singapore

Preface

The present study was sponsored within the framework of an on-going ARTEP project on Employment, Income Distribution and Poverty in Asian countries. A principal objective of the project is to analyse changes over time in income distribution and poverty and the determinants and characteristics of poverty in different socio-economic settings. This will involve, among other things, studies on the experience of developing countries in Asia, especially the socialist transformation of agrarian institutions.

It is hoped that the present study, based on the results of the analysis of an extensive body of original data collected by the authors during a field-trip to China in 1979, will constitute a significant contribution towards understanding the experience of a major Asian country in dealing with a dominant objective of economic development — that of combining growth and equality in the rural economy.

ARTEP

Acknowledgements

The results reported in this monograph are based on data collected on a field trip to China in 1979. The trip was financed by the George Webb Medley Fund of Oxford University and by the Overseas Development Administration. We are particularly grateful to Robert Porter of ODA for his encouragement and support.

Our hosts in China were the Institute of Agricultural Economics of the Chinese Academy of Social Sciences. We owe a great deal to our friends in the Institute and to the accountants, cadres and authorities at national and provincial levels who cooperated with us so fully in answering questions and providing data.

The Asian Regional Team for Employment Promotion of the International Labour Organization supported the preparation of this study. We are grateful to A.R. Khan, the Director of ARTEP, and to E.L.H. Lee for their assistance and helpful comments. Ashok Rudra and Nicholas Lardy also provided helpful comments and suggestions. Computational assistance was provided by Setareh Alavi-Moghadam and the numerous drafts were typed by Muriel Payne. We are grateful to them both.

Oxford   K.B.G.
April 1981   A.S.

Contents

one

Introductory Remarks

The Trip

On 11 June 1979, six members of Queen Elizabeth House, Oxford arrived in Beijing to begin a study tour of rural China. In addition to ourselves, the delegation included Roger Hay, Marsh Marshall, Neville Maxwell and Peter Nolan. The main purpose of the trip was to learn at first hand about the new policies that had recently been introduced to promote rural development and to discover, if we could, what the likely consequences would be. One of the controversial issues raised by the new policies was their possible effects on the distribution of income in the countryside, particularly at the local level. The two of us decided to make this issue the focal point of our research.

Our host in China was the Chinese Academy of Social Sciences (CASS) and its Vice-President, Mr. Huan Xiang, went out of his way to facilitate our investigations. CASS consists of 21 research institutes, of which five are concerned with various aspects of economics. We were attached to the Institute of Agricultural Economics, the organization directly concerned with the subject of our enquiries.

The Institute of Agricultural Economics was only a year old at the time of our arrival. It had been created shortly after the overthrow of the "Gang of Four", during a period when China began to revitalize her universities and research establishments after the upheavals of the Cultural Revolution. The Institute made all the arrangements for our three field trips and interviews with national, provincial and local officials. The Vice-Director of the Institute, Mr. Wang Geng-Jin, accompanied us throughout our travels and was a pleasant companion and a valuable source of information. He worked tirelessly on our behalf and was instrumental in making it possible for us to obtain a large

1

amount of quantitative material at the communes we visited.

Our work began in Beijing with a meeting with Mr. Zheng Zhong, the Vice-Minister for Agriculture. Mr. Zheng briefed us on the government's current thinking on agriculture. He talked at some length about the need to improve incentives to work harder (through greater reliance on "payment according to work") and to increase output (through higher grain prices). He talked, too, of the government's intention to stabilize the three-tier level of ownership in the commune and in particular of the decision to confirm the production team as the accounting unit. It was government policy, he said, to concentrate on the modernization of agriculture through greater investment in irrigation, fertilizer, electricity and agricultural equipment. Although this might lead to some increase in income inequality, the changes were not expected to be very large and the government was not unduly concerned about them. He regarded the relationship between collective ownership and private activities as harmonious and foresaw an important role for rural markets as an outlet for surplus production. It was the intention of the government to provide material and technical assistance to the peasantry in order to strengthen their political support for the government. Many of the policy issues raised by the Vice-Minister for Agriculture clearly are central to this study and we shall return to them at numerous points throughout this book.

The next thing we did in China, on 13 June, was to visit Evergreen People's Commune in the Beijing Municipality. This was our first encounter with the country's collective agricultural system. Evergreen People's Commune is a rich commune close to the capital. It has become a famous showpiece and receives many visitors every year both from abroad and other parts of China. It was formed in August 1958 and has a population of about 43,000. It has 2,667 ha. of cultivated land on which it grows mostly vegetables. Indeed, over 100 varieties of vegetables are grown on 1,667 ha. In addition, there are 400 ha. of orchards (apples, peaches, pears and grapes) and 600 ha. of wheat, rice and maize. There are 48,000 pigs, i.e., more pigs than people, 40,000 ducks plus chickens, bees and oxen. The commune contains 12 factories and workshops plus a construction team which between them employ nearly 23 per cent of the labour force and account for 60 per cent of the commune's income.

The households on the commune own their own homes, which are well built. Education is free and universal at primary and middle school levels. The hospital with a staff of more than 100 and the 14 clinics with 200 "barefoot" doctors provide a free medical service. Kindergartens and nurseries also are free, as incidentally are films. There are 56 days of maternity leave to mothers on full pay. The age of retirement is the same as in Britain, namely, age 60 for women and 65 for men; the pension is roughly equivalent to half normal earnings. Evergreen, evidently, is far from a typical rural commune, but it does show what can be done under ideal conditions. It was a good, if brief, introduction to the best that China has been able to offer so far to its rural population.

The next day we took a train to Shijiazhuang, the provincial capital of Hebei Province. The province, whose name means "north of the Yellow

River'', is fairly typical of northern China. It has a continental climate with hot summers and cold winters; rainfall is moderate and restricted to the summer; dust storms are common in the spring. The province occasionally suffers from serious drought, as happened in 1980. The most important crop is wheat, which is planted in winter and followed by maize in the summer. The province is Ch' a's largest producer of cotton and an important producer of peanuts and ot .r oilseed crops as well.

After meeting provincial officials and obtaining from them background data on the province as a whole, we boarded a microbus for the journey to Wu Gong Commune. The commune consists of ten production brigades, of which one — Wu Gong Brigade — has been designated a "model brigade". The population of the commune is 16,500 and the labour force is 7,200, most of whom are engaged in growing wheat and peanuts. Thanks to the generosity of the commune's accountants we were able to obtain a complete set of Wu Gong's production and financial data and the reader will notice that these data occupy a prominent position in our analysis.

We were so impressed by our field observations in Wu Gong that we began to worry that perhaps the commune was a bit too much of a "model" and consequently was not really representative of a typical middle income commune in north China. Accordingly we asked to visit the neighbouring commune, Qie Ma Commune, and to use it to check our findings at Wu Gong. This was readily agreed by our hosts. In the event, our worries turned out to be unfounded.

At Qie Ma we were met by the Vice-Chairman, a woman, and told that we could have whatever information we needed for our research. The commune is a little larger than Wu Gong. Its population is 19,466 and the labour force is 9,220. The cropping pattern is similar to that at Wu Gong, as is the range of industrial and sideline activities. All the land is irrigated and devoted to wheat, maize, millet and cotton.

One distinguishing feature of Qie Ma — and of most of the brigades of Wu Gong Commune — was that the private plots are planted to grain and collectively farmed by the teams. The produce, of course, is distributed directly to members of the team, but unlike the usual practice whereby households cultivate their own private plots, in Qie Ma, this is done collectively. The effect of this is to eliminate private cultivation while retaining private ownership of the produce. The significance of the latter, in turn, is that private produce is not subject to taxation by the state. In other words, private plots have been abolished in practice in Qie Ma although they have been retained in name only in order to minimize liability to taxation. This is a good example of the pragmatic approach most Chinese take to political and economic questions.

The grain pricing system is another example of pragmatism in action. The government was anxious to maintain adequate supplies of grain for the urban areas through its quota delivery system while providing greater price incentives on the margin to stimulate production and above quota sales. These two objectives were reconciled in practice through a multiple pricing system. First, in the autumn of 1979, sales to the state of top quality wheat under the quota system occurred at a price of 0.36 yuan per kilo. Next, additional sales under the county's annual purchasing plan enjoyed a 50 per cent price premium, viz., 0.54 yuan per kilo. Then voluntary additional sales above the annual purchasing plan (sometimes known as "discussion grain") enjoyed a price premium that was subject to negotiation and could be as high as 100 per cent, i.e., a price per kilo of 0.72 yuan. Lastly, a production team (or a household) could sell collective (or private) grain on the free market. The price on the free market usually was only slightly higher than the variable price for voluntary sales and this presumably reflected mostly transaction costs. In addition, the free market was used for the disposal of lower quality grains.

Having completed our enquiries in Hebei Province, we returned to Beijing to meet Vice-Premier Deng Xiaoping on 21 June. We were granted an interview of well over an hour with the Vice-Premier and engaged in a frank and lively exchange of views. All of us were greatly impressed by Deng's command of the facts, his grasp of policy issues and the uncompromising position he adopted towards his critics. At the end of the discussion some members of our delegation feared that Deng was interested only in growth and was little concerned with distributive issues. Others interpreted his remarks to mean that he intended to place greater emphasis on increasing production but would take steps to prevent inequalities from becoming unacceptably wide.

The different interpretations within our group about the relationship between agricultural growth and income distribution increased our interest in studying both a poor and an exceptionally rich commune. So it was with enthusiasm that the next day we flew to Shanghai to visit Cheng Dong Commune in Jia Ding County, Shanghai Municipality, a rich commune which, moreover, was in an area where the influence of the Gang of Four was said to have been strong. This gave an extra dimension to our research.

Shanghai Municipality is located at the mouth of the Yangtse River on the eastern tip of Jiangsu Province. Shanghai is the largest city in China and is the nation's industrial and commercial centre. The rural communes located in the four counties that comprise the municipality are probably the most prosperous in China. Certainly yields are higher in the municipality than anywhere else in the country and grain usually is tripple cropped, i.e., two crops of rice followed by one of wheat. Cotton is important and, of course, vegetables are cultivated very intensively. The transportation network based on canals is excellent.

Cheng Dong Commune conforms to the above general description quite well. It has a population of 25,626 and a labour force of about 16,000. The cultivated area is 1,761 ha., of which 90 per cent is irrigated. The cropping ratio consequently is high at 2.3. There are 17 Production Brigades in the commune including one which specializes in fishing and pearl cultivation. There are a very large number of commune level industries and in fact 46.6 per cent of the commune's total income in 1978 was generated at the commune level; only 27.5 per cent was generated in the essentially agricultural activities at the team level.

The history of the commune can be traced back to late 1950 and the spring of 1951 when the land was confiscated and redistributed to poor peasants. The beneficiaries of the land reform then formed mutual aid groups and by the end of 1953 there were 333 such groups. Elementary cooperatives were formed in 1954: the land was pooled and output was divided, 60 per cent used as payment for labour and 40 per cent set aside as rent for the use of land. In 1955, there were 80 of these elementary cooperatives. Advanced cooperatives, in which payment for land ceased, were formed during the subsequent period, and by 1956 – 57 there were 12 advanced cooperatives. The present commune was established in 1958 from the 12 advanced cooperatives. Until 1962 the brigades were the basic accounting unit, but in that year the level of account was reduced to the team. In 1977, three brigades decided to raise the level of account again, but at the time of our visit one of these brigades was considering reverting to the earlier pattern and lowering the level of account once again to the production team.

Cheng Dong has experimented not only with raising the level of account and greater centralization but also with more decentralization and breaking the teams up into work groups. Since 1978, there have been 28 Production Teams (out of a total of 150 teams) which specify quotas for work groups. Typically in such cases the team is divided into two to five work groups. In some teams a work group is given a specific task with its specific number of work points, e.g., a harvesting task. It is then the responsibility of the group to complete the task and divide the work points among the members of the group. In other teams a specific task with a fixed number of work points is assigned to an individual. An example would be collecting a boat load of silt from the river to be used as fertilizer. This is essentially a piece rate system of payment. Still other teams use a time rate payment system combined with an assessment of the intensity of effort and the quality of the work performed. These various payment systems often are used simultaneously within a team depending on the nature of the task to be undertaken.

Xu Jia Team of Li Xin Brigade is divided into two work groups, each with 39 workers and 110.5 mou of land (about 7.7 ha.). Each work group is responsible for cultivating its own land although the team keeps the equipment and lends it to the work groups as required. Each work group has a fixed production quota for each crop, and the quota is the same for each group because they are picked in such a way that they are of equal strength.

Once a year a mass meeting of Xu Jia Team decides on the composition of the work groups, with the intention of ensuring that both work groups have the same number of strong and weak workers. Similarly, the mass meeting decides on the allocation of land. Changes typically are marginal, but the composition of the groups does change, e.g., because of demographic changes. The allocation of land remains essentially unchanged but work groups are allowed to help each other for payment in work points. In some cases, moreover, the work groups are themselves divided into smaller groups. For instance, in 1978, the work groups were divided in two for the cotton crop, making four groups in all below the level of the team.

The danger of this practice is that it could gradually undermine the team as the level of account and destroy the institution on which collective agriculture has been based in China. If this were to occur it would be a reactionary step in the literal sense of being a movement backwards towards a more elementary form of cooperation that was superseded in Cheng Dong a quarter of a century ago. Having identified this danger, however, it must be said that the work groups in Cheng Dong did not appear to be a threat to the three-tiered system of collective organization in the commune. Reports from other regions of China, on the other hand, suggest that the threat is real.

Our last "squat" was in Tang Tang People's Commune, a much poorer commune in Guangdong, the southernmost province of China. Guangdong is a rice and sugarcane producing region with a hot, wet and humid climate. The two main agricultural areas of the province are the Pearl River delta and the island of Hainan. The commune we visited, however, was in Fo Gang County, a less prosperous part of the province some distance north of the delta and of Guangzhou (Canton), the provincial capital. In contrast to Jia Ding County in the Shanghai Municipality, Fo Gang is almost entirely rural. In fact, of a total population in 1978 of 222,182, almost 95 per cent are classified as rural. Similarly, in contrast to Cheng Dong, Tang Tang Commune has only a small industrial sector; most of the commune's income originates in agriculture and forestry, and 74 per cent of collective income is produced at the level of the team. The main crops are rice and, far behind, wheat. The population of the commune is 35,100.

As in Shanghai, so too in Fo Gang there are work groups. In the county as a whole there are 1,642 production teams, of which 112 or less than 7 per cent have work groups. In Tang Tang, the proportion is much higher: 47 out of the 235 teams have work groups, i.e., exactly 20 per cent. In the majority of cases, however, the smallest unit of cooperative labour is the team.

Each member of the team accumulates work points, and a record is kept both by the individual himself and by a person designated by the team. Points are recorded daily and a summary is prepared once a month. Work points are allocated by the team on the basis of fixed work quotas in most instances. For example, one might receive 40 work points for transplanting one mou[1] of rice in one team, and either a smaller or larger number of points in another team. Norms also are used, particularly in cases where labour cannot easily be evaluated on a piece-work basis, but there is no doubt that in Tang Tang the quota system is more popular.

There are 27,000 pigs raised in the commune, most of them, viz. 24,600, privately. The economics of this private activity is curious and illustrates how the state has encouraged the household economy to produce more pig meat as a source of protein and more pig manure as a source of organic fertilizer.

All privately raised pigs in Tang Tang must be sold to the state. However, half of the pig is returned to the household either in kind or in the form of meat

---

[1] 1 mou = one-sixth acre.

coupons. This has been provincial policy since 1977. The price received by the farmer for his pig is 0.807 yuan per jin or 1.614 yuan per kilo. In addition, the household is allowed to buy from the state 15 kilos of rice at a total price of about three yuan. Next, for each pig raised, the household is entitled to 0.03 mou of land for fodder. In practice, this land is enough to provide 50 – 60 per cent of the fodder needed to raise a pig; much of the remaining fodder can be obtained by cutting grass in the mountains. Note that this land for pig raising is additional to the land allocated to households as private plots, which in Tang Tang is equal to 0.05 mou per head. Finally, pig manure can be sold by the household to the team for work points, which ultimately of course are payable in grain or cash. The various transactions surrounding pig production are rather complex, but our rough calculations suggest that the state provides a very large subsidy to private pig raising. Indeed, it is possible that from the point of view of the household, the whole of the revenue is value added or income. That is, the material costs of pig raising are nearly zero.

The state, then, subsidizes private pig raising and this has led to an enormous increase in the pig population of the country since 1949. At the same time, the state recently has increased grain prices in order to encourage greater output and sales. The two policies may be in partial conflict in that on the margin an expansion of the pig (and poultry) population is likely to lead to a diversion of grain into animal feed, a reduction in grain sales (especially of coarse grains) and consequently to grain shortages in some urban areas. In the long run, of course, higher prices for grains should stimulate production and thereby permit both an expansion of the animal population and higher direct grain consumption in urban areas. In the short run, however, when total supplies of grain are fixed, there may be awkward transitional problems.

Observations on Our Research Methods

Before describing the contents of the book, the reader should know something about our approach to research on rural China. There are many ways of treating a subject and no single method is clearly superior to all others. All we can do is indicate the characteristic features of our approach and hope that the reader will judge them to have been appropriate in the circumstances. There are perhaps five points that are worth making.

First, the reader will notice that in analyzing growth and distributional issues in rural China, we make few references to other works on this theme and refrain from discussing them, except briefly in passing. This does not imply that the writings of other authors are without merit or that we reject their findings. Rather it reflects the fact that ours is not a work of synthesis but one which attempts to add fresh materials to this important topic and to employ new methods of analysis. Moreover, in the course of our field work, we were able to obtain enough statistical material to allow us to investigate these issues in some detail without having to rely on data supplied by other investigators. Since the data on rural China are not standardized and sometimes are difficult to interpret, our approach helped us to avoid the errors that inevitably would arise from using data collected for other purposes from communes with which we were unfamiliar.

Second, the book is written from the vantage point of political economy. That is, we observed rural China not through the eyes of general Sinologists but through those of applied development economists. This would not have been possible a few years ago in China and thus our study benefited from and is one of the indirect effects of the process of liberalization of contacts with tne West. It also reflects, of course, the new policies of the Chinese government towards international research and academic exchanges with foreign scholars.

These new policies are likely to lead to a transformation of the study of contemporary China in the West. The significance of the China-watchers in Hong Kong and elsewhere is likely to decline and the handicap that comes from not knowing the Chinese language will almost certainly be greatly diminished. This is particularly true of applied economic research based on quantitative information. Ready access to such data already has begun to have two implications for the study of the Chinese economy. Firstly, it has become possible to pursue lines of enquiry which formerly were very difficult if not impossible because of insufficient statistical material. Secondly, because these materials now are more readily available, it has become possible to use techniques of analysis which formerly could not be applied. The reader will find that our book illustrates both these points. On the other hand, it is probable that the book contains weaknesses which would have been avoided had the authors been traditional Sinologists. We hope, however, that our methods of analysis will constitute some contribution to the state of the art.

Third, we have tried as far as possible to avoid inserting our study into a preselected ideological framework. We were able to do this, to the extent that we succeeded, because of the large amount of statistical material that was made available to us. This enabled us to follow a more empirical line of enquiry than might otherwise have been possible. This does not imply that the approach of the empiricist is always better than other approaches, but we believe that at this stage of research into the Chinese economy it is important to establish the empirical contours within which ideological debates can be situated and propositions tested. An overall political evaluation of China's performance ultimately cannot be avoided, but we do not feel that we learned enough from our field investigations to be able now to make a general assessment of the country.

This brings us to our fourth point: the scope of this study. The shortness of the trip forced us to focus on a limited number of themes; in order to be effective, we had to be selective. At the same time we did benefit from being part of a larger group working with several interpreters in that we were able to acquire a larger perspective and place our own investigations into a wider context. Nevertheless, we have chosen to stay within the confines of our selected topic of growth and equality in rural China except in the final section of the book, where we enlarge our horizon to encompass wider issues.

Perhaps a more significant self-imposed constraint is that we have deliberately chosen not to use as evidence reports that have appeared since we returned from China in July 1979. That is, we have relied on our own observations, on the data we were given or collected ourselves and on information provided in face-to-face discussions with responsible officials whom we could identify. This method of research obviously has some limitations. For example, some of the measures that were in force in China when we were there have since been altered. Indeed, some changes will be obvious to the informed reader. To the extent that this has happened, our conclusions may not be wholly valid. Moreover, by excluding from consideration reports which have appeared since our visit, we are able to speak with less authority about the direction in which things are moving in rural China. We have a snapshot of rural China taken in the summer of 1979; we are reluctant to try to make a film of rural China by splicing to our snapshot other photographs taken in different places, at different times by different photographers. To this extent, our conclusions are circumscribed, but we hope that by opting for restricted but firm evidence, our conclusions will carry greater validity.

Finally, we must say something about the authenticity of our field observations. The reader is entitled to ask whether we were shown only show-pieces and unrepresentative communes or whether what we saw and heard and measured was indeed indicative of conditions in the rural areas.

Let us begin with an outline of the process through which we came to visit the particular units that we studied, rather than others. The choice of the regions to be studied, and within these of the types of communes to be studied was made by us and was agreed by our hosts. Our hosts then made the choice of the actual communes to be visited. Once at the commune, usually we were invited to visit selected units within it. However, at this and subsequent stages we were given ample opportunity to modify the provisional programme made for us. In the end, we chose the brigades and the teams to be visited after a careful and often lengthy scrutiny of the financial records of the units. We were assisted in this selection process by the provision of the relevant statistics by the leaders and accountants of the units concerned. The Chinese, far from being obstructive, actively assisted us to select units which conformed as closely as possible to our criteria. In general, we attempted to visit a rich unit, a poor unit and other units which had characteristics of special interest.

Whether or not the units we studied were "representative" depends partly on one's notion of typicality. Given the enormous variation in conditions in rural China, it is not clear what an "average" or "representative" commune would be. None the less, it is a legitimate fear that we might have been exposed only to relatively rich communes without realizing it. We attempted to remove this anxiety by calibrating the income levels of the different units we visited on a national scale. That is, when we visited a production team, we would situate it within the spread of incomes of the other teams of the brigade. Similarly, we would place the brigade within the income spread at the commune level. We also obtained county level and provincial data, so that if we did visit a relatively rich unit, we were immediately aware of this fact and could take it into account when making judgements.

Having said this, however, our calibrations do show that most of the communes we visited were indeed average or above average ones in terms of their per capita distributed collective income. On the other hand, a great many brigades and teams that we subsequently selected for study were clearly relatively poor. To some extent the bias against the less well off communes arose from the fact that the regions we visited were not among the poorest ones. In addition, there is a perfectly understandable desire on the part of the Chinese to show outsiders communes which have achieved average levels of income or better. Perhaps it is unrealistic to expect to be able to correct for this bias in the course of one short trip.

In a planned future visit, we hope to study a group of poor communes in regions some distance from the developed coastal provinces. If this trip does occur, it will give us an opportunity to observe communes at very different levels of income. For the purposes of this book, however, the question of the representativeness of the communes visited is of secondary importance. The reason for this is that a major part of the analysis is concerned with the processes determining growth and distribution within communes, not among communes. That is, our focus is at the grass roots level of the brigade and team.

One of the units we visited, namely Wu Gong Production Brigade, was indeed a "model" and was displayed not just to outsiders like ourselves but also to visiting delegations from other parts of China. In this instance we were able to convert the apparent disadvantage of Wu Gong Brigade of not being "representative" into an advantage. That is, we could study in great detail how a "model brigade" functions, how it had developed in recent times and what role was played in the growth process by local initiative. Moreover, by comparing Wu Gong Brigade with the other brigades of Wu Gong Commune, which were not models, we could determine the degree to which the model brigade had been elevated above its neighbours and observe how all the brigades co-existed within the framework of the parent commune. These aspects of our enquiries, however, are not discussed in the chapters that follow. Instead we concentrate on the interrelationships between economic development and income distribution in rural China.

An Outline of the Book

Part One of this book is concerned with the pattern of income inequality in rural China. In Chapter 2 we present our data on the distribution of collective income in the countryside. This is largely descriptive and is intended to demonstrate the high degree of equality that has been achieved. In Chapter 3 we concentrate on two things. First, we show that in many cases the distribution of income has tended over time gradually to become more equal. Second, we suggest that there are forces operating inside the commune system which account for this. That is, we argue that the commune system as presently organized contains an endogenous mechanism which tends to lead to a reduction in inequality.

In addition to the endogenous forces, there are three other factors which, in practice, have led to a more equal distribution of income. One of these is the allocation of jobs in the industrial sector in county, provincial and state manufacturing establishments outside the commune. A second is the systematic transfer of capital in the form of grants and loans to poor brigades and teams. The third is the role played by the household economy. We argue that the private sector has been inserted into the socialist economy in such a way that, at least at the local level, private economic activities often tend to raise the income of poor households above what they otherwise would have been and in this way reduce inequalities in per capita consumption.

In Part Two we examine in great detail the process of equalizing growth in a Chinese commune. Using data from Wu Gong and Cheng Dong, we attempt to construct a model which captures the essential features determining the distribution of collective income within a commune over time. This simulation model abstracts from policy changes and ignores the equalizing role of capital transfers, the private sector and employment outside the commune. That is, the model focuses entirely on the internal dynamics of the collective sector.

The components of the model are discussed in Chapter 5. A key role is shown to be played by what we call the aggregate productivity relationship, a statistical function describing the connection between material inputs and the resulting flow of output. Our evidence indicates there is a strong tendency for the productivity of material inputs to decline as levels of application increase. The implication of this is that if inputs are distributed equally on the margin, brigades and teams with relatively low levels of output and income will expand more rapidly than brigades and teams with high levels of output. That is, the aggregate productivity relationship operates in such a way that initial differences in the distribution of income gradually are reduced.

We also consider direct taxation and the relationship between fixed and working capital. In both cases these are shown to be of minor significance. The savings function or collective accumulation relationship, in contrast, is very important. Our evidence indicates that the savings behaviour of communes in China is broadly Keynesian. That is, the richer the brigade or team the higher the proportion of income that is saved and invested. This implies that richer units will accumulate capital at a faster pace than poorer ones and consequently, everything else being equal, they will tend to grow faster. These differences in rates of accumulation and growth will tend over time to lead to an increase in income inequality, unless of course they are compensated by a policy of transferring capital to poor units.

The various components of the model are assembled in Chapter 6. We argue that changes in the distribution of income depend on the balance of two conflicting forces. If the effects of the aggregate productivity relationship outweigh those of the accumulation relationship, inequality will tend to decline; if not, inequality will tend to rise. The issue is an empirical rather than a theoretical one. In practice, our simulations indicate that in the long run inequality does tend to decline. Moreover, this finding is rather robust in the sense that it is not very sensitive to changes in assumptions. In the short run, however, the outcome is not so predictable. Usually, inequality in the distribution of collective income begins to fall immediately, but in some trials inequality first increased (sometimes substantially) before beginning to decline. In every case the degree of inequality was lower after 50 years than it was initially. Indeed, with only three exceptions, inequality was lower after 20 years than it was initially and in all but 20 out of 180 cases it was lower after ten years. Clearly there are powerful forces operating independently of government policy interventions which contribute to the creation of a more equal society in the Chinese countryside.

This does not mean, of course, that public policy is of little importance. Indeed we devote the whole of Part Three to policy questions and strategies for economic development in rural China. We begin in Chapter 7 with four topics: the institutional framework, the overall distribution of income and wealth, regional inequalities and rural-urban income differentials. In Chapter 8 we turn to three sector issues: employment in agriculture, rural industrialization and policies to control the rate of increase of the population. In the final chapter we discuss the policies of the "Gang of Four" as they applied to rural areas and then conclude with a few speculations on the direction in which present policies may be moving.

PART ONE

THE PATTERN OF INCOME INEQUALITY
IN RURAL CHINA

two

The Distribution of Income

The distribution of income in China has long been a subject of interest. Unfortunately, however, because of insufficient quantitative information, it has not been possible to assess accurately the degree of equality that has been achieved. Instead we have had to be content with rather impressionistic descriptive studies and empirical analyses based on fragmentary evidence. Happily this situation is changing and it is now possible to shed a great deal more light on many issues related to equity and growth.

In Part One we attempt to do three things. First, we attempt to measure the distribution of income in rural China, relying heavily on data on the distribution of collective income in the rural areas of Hebei and Guangdong provinces. Second, we examine the determinants of inequality in rural areas and where possible we measure them. Third, anticipating a bit the lengthy analysis in Part Two, we discuss the inter-relationships between rural development and the distribution of collective income. Thus we are concerned with measuring the extent of inequality, determining its structure at any moment in time and analyzing the dynamic forces which affect it over time.

Our study is concerned with the Chinese countryside. The urban areas are excluded and hence important rural-urban inequalities fall outside our purview. While this is a significant omission, it should not be forgotten that over four-fifths of China's population lives in rural areas and thus are included within our analysis. Except where the contrary is indicated, we focus on total rural income and not just on agricultural production. That is, the concept of income we employ covers net output from crop production and forestry, animal husbandry and fishing, and the so-called sideline occupations of rural industry, construction and handicrafts. Remittances from urban areas, however, are not included.

15

At the commune and intra-commune levels, our data refer generally to the distributed component of collective income. This excludes collective savings and also non-collective income. The latter could take the form of earnings or remittances of workers employed outside the commune, and also household level earnings from private economic activities. Some of these aspects are discussed later, but it is appropriate to record now the nature of the biases that each of these omissions is likely to impart to the level of inequality reported below.

The exclusion of remittances generates one known and one unknown bias. To the extent that outside employment is rationed — formally or informally — in favour of the poorer teams (or households), our use of distributed collective income probably has the effect of exaggerating the degree of inequality in the distribution of consumption among the units concerned. An opposite bias would operate to the extent that the economically stronger units managed to "compete" more successfully for these lucrative jobs outside the commune. This is an empirically resolvable question, and the answer might well be that such jobs are randomly distributed. On the other hand, the employment of an adult member of a household outside the commune would *ipso facto* lead to a reduction in that household's labour units earning collective income within the commune. The statistics for distributed collective income, far from showing this as an advantaged household, would show it as being poorer than a similar household which had its entire labour force employed within the commune. This implies a definitional upward bias to our statistics of inequality, but since it is generally felt that inequality in rural China is remarkably low, it is important that any biases should be in an upward direction.

Our data do not include income from the private sector. That is, we focus almost exclusively on collective rural income. Field observations suggest that private rural income — from pig raising and poultry, household plots, wood gathering, handicrafts, etc., but not including imputed rents from privately owned houses — can account for as much as 40 per cent of household income and perhaps for as much as 20 per cent on average. Moreover, it is our impression that within a given commune, income from private sector economic activities tends on balance to reduce inter-household inequality below what it otherwise would have been. The reason for this is that opportunities in the private sector are exploited most intensively by two types of households, namely, those with an above average number of elderly persons and those with an above average number of infants. In the case of the former, the private sector enables the old to generate an income and contribute to the household despite the fact that they are too infirm to engage in collective agricultural labour. In the case of the latter, private sector activities enable mothers with young children to continue earning an income despite the fact that their maternal responsibilities deprive them of an opportunity to engage in full-time collective activities. The children can also make useful contributions of labour. Thus the importance of the private sector varies over the life cycle and, in effect, the private sector allows households with an unfavourable dependency ratio to compensate for this. Consequently, by excluding the private sector, we probably have exaggerated the degree of intra-commune inequality in the distribution of income among households in rural China. That is, once again, our measures of inequality probably are biased upwards. As explained before, this is as it should be.

In an all-China context, in contrast, private sector incomes may not be equalizing. The reason for this is that communes located near prosperous urban areas probably have opportunities to acquire private incomes from the sale of handicrafts, vegetables, pigs and other farm produce to urban residents. These opportunities would not exist, or would exist in lesser degree, in communes less favourably located.

It should be noted, however, that while the *distributed* component of collective income is an appropriate measure — after due account is taken of non-collective sources — if one is interested in studying present household consumption levels, the *total* collective income measure is more appropriate for the analysis of growth and, therefore, of future consumption levels. Since a higher proportion of collective income is likely to be accumulated at higher levels of income, the distributed collective income figures will understate the inter-unit differentials from the growth point of view, while the total collective income profile is likely to overstate the differentials from the point of view of consumption levels. This can be illustrated by using the inter-brigade data for Wu Gong Commune: the ratio of the highest to the lowest brigade distributed collective income average is 2.85 while the ratio for total (net) collective income is 3.11. The two richest brigades save 32 and 45 per cent of their total collective income, while the poorest manages only 25 per cent. The present point refers, of course, to the choice of the appropriate income measure, rather than to any statistical bias in the measure adopted.

The data for our research were supplied to us by provincial and county officials and by accountants at the communes, brigades and teams we visited. Field work was concentrated in three areas: Wu Gong Commune in Hebei Province, a wheat growing region; Cheng Dong Commune in the Shanghai Municipality, a prosperous commune in Jia Ding County which produces both agricultural and industrial products for the great metropolis; and Tang Tang Commune in Guangdong Province, a relatively poor commune in Fo Gang County which grows rice in terraced fields. In addition, to supplement the information from our case studies, data were obtained from a few other areas, e.g., Evergreen Commune in the Beijing Municipality, Qie Ma Commune in Hebei and aggregate data from Shanghai County in the Shanghai Municipality. Thus we have evidence from North, Central and South China, the areas where the population is concentrated, but nothing from the more backward regions of West China. Similarly, in the areas and communes visited, we have cases of rich, poor and middle-income units. On the whole, however, we believe our data are representative essentially of the conditions in which the majority of the people live in the middle and upper-middle regions of the income distribution in rural China. Rather than make possibly indefensible claims that the regions and units we visited were representative in some general sense, we are content to note that each unit we visited and from which we gathered statistics can be situated in its proper context and compared with higher level units using the same income variable.

Income Distribution in Hebei Province

Let us begin by considering in some detail the distribution of income in Hebei Province. Hebei is one of the most populous provinces in northern China and is larger, in fact, than Vietnam, Thailand or the Philippines. In 1978, the rural population was 44.8 million, of which 17 million were in the labour force. Average household size is 4.3 persons and the dependency ratio, i.e. the number of non-workers that must be supported by each member of the labour force, is 1.6. The basic data are summarized in Table 2:1.

Between them, crop production and sideline occupations account for just over 90 per cent of rural income. Crop production alone accounts for 65 per cent of total income, the most important crop being wheat, followed by cotton and oil bearing crops. Sideline occupations account for 26 per cent. Forestry (2.3 per cent) and animal husbandry (1.5 per cent) are of marginal significance only. In terms of its income level, Hebei is an average province, though compared to central and southern China, it is rather poor, primarily because irrigation is not extensive and hence agriculture still is heavily dependent on a single rainfed crop a year.

Distributed collective income per head in 1978 was 75.74 yuan. (The official exchange rate is US$1 = 1.52 yuan.) There is of course some dispersion around this average, but if one compares the richest with the poorest county in the province, it transpires that the ratio of the highest to lowest per capita county (xian) income is a relatively modest 4.78.

Table 2:1 Basic Data: Hebei Province, 1978

1.	Rural population	44,774,000
2.	Rural labour force	17,030,000
3.	Rural households	10,390,000
4.	Average size of household	4.31
5.	Workers per household	1.64
6.	Dependency ratio	1.63
7.	Composition of collective rural income (%)	
	Crops	64.7
	Forestry	2.3
	Animal husbandry	1.5
	Sideline occupations	26.2
	Fishing	0.4
	Miscellaneous	4.8
8.	Per capita collective income (yuan)	75.74
9.	Ratio of highest to lowest per capita county (xian) income	4.78

It is possible to say a great deal more than this, however, about the distribution of income in Hebei. Data are available on income distribution by income intervals for both the 247,788 Production Teams in the province and the 148 counties. These data are reported in Table 2:2. It can be seen at a glance that the distribution is remarkably even. The mean per capita income and the mode coincide, while the upper tail of the distribution accounts for only a small fraction of the observations.

Notice that the number of counties that are very poor, i.e. with a per capita income of 40 yuan or less, is insignificant compared to the proportion of teams that are very poor. Specifically, 13.9 per cent of the teams in the province have a per capita distributed collective income of 40 yuan or less, whereas only 1.4 per cent of the counties are that poor on average. Assuming the number of teams per county does not vary widely, this implies that the observed degree of inequality cannot be described in terms of geographical factors alone. Indeed, very poor teams, i.e. those with a per capita income of less than 41 yuan, are more or less randomly distributed through space.

Table 2:2 Per Capita Collective Income in Hebei Province, 1978

Per Capita income (yuan)	No. of Production Teams	Percentage of Teams	No. of Counties	Percentage of Counties
0 – 40	34,331	13.9	2	1.4
41 – 50	35,009	14.1	15	10.1
51 – 60	34,937	14.0	19	12.8
61 – 80	58,633	23.7	54	36.4
81 – 100	42,253	17.1	39	26.4
101 – 150	36,569	14.8	17	11.5
more than 150	6,056	2.4	2	1.4

This is an important conclusion. One might expect that in an area as large and populous as Hebei, regional inequalities would be more evident. The 190,000 km² of the province are divided into three distinct zones: the north and west are hilly, the centre and south consist of plains, while in the east the soil is sandy and alkaline. If such regional geographical differences were the major source of inequality between units, we would expect to find a greater identity between the team and the county distributions. But since poor teams are not generally all clustered in the poor counties, the implication is that there are important factors in addition to geographical attributes which influence the inter-team, and hence inter-county, inequality in incomes. Some of these factors, such as different land-man ratios, irrigation and industrial facilities will be alluded to later. It would of course be rash to generalize from Hebei to China as a whole — indeed inter-regional differences are bound to be large in a country that includes both Tibet and Shanghai Municipality — but the evidence so far suggests that there is more to regional inequality in rural China than differences in climate, topography and natural resources.

Unfortunately, we are unable to compare the income of teams with those of counties in the other provinces we studied and hence there is little more that can be said about intra-provincial regional inequality. We do have data, however, on the incomes of the 297,100 Production Teams in the province of Guangdong and this enables us to compare the distribution among teams in two major provinces, one in the north and the other in the south. The data for Guangdong are reproduced in Table 2:3.

Table 2:3 Per Capita Collective Income in Guangdong Province, 1978

Per Capita Income (yuan)	No. of Production Teams	Percentage of Teams
0 – 40	55,400	18.7
41 – 50	43,300	14.6
51 – 100	150,600	50.7
101 – 150	33,000	11.1
more than 150	14,800	4.9

The model per capita collective income for both provinces falls in the 51 – 100 yuan size-class, and the estimated per capita collective income for Guangdong is 73.4 yuan, just 2.3 yuan less than the Hebei figure. However, the distributions suggest that inequality is somewhat greater in Guangdong. This is evident from the fact that a higher proportion of teams in Guangdong are in the lowest interval and have a per capita income of 40 yuan or less. Equally, a higher proportion of teams are in the top interval and have a per capita income of more than 150 yuan a year. Nevertheless, the distribution of income in the two provinces is quite similar, on the whole; it would be interesting to see if data for other provinces reveal similar distribution profiles.

The data for Hebei can be reorganized and displayed as a decile ranking, as is done in Table 2:4 for both counties and teams. This has the advantage of presenting the information in a way which is familiar and which permits comparison with other societies.

The remarkable equality in the distribution of income in rural Hebei province is readily apparent, and the comparison with many other Third World countries is stark. It is not uncommon, for example, for the top 10 per cent of recipients in the Third World to account for as much as 40 per cent of total income, whereas in Hebei the richest decile of production teams receives only 18 per cent of the distributed collective income. Similarly, in many poor countries, the bottom 40 per cent of the population may receive as little as 10 per cent of total income, whereas in Hebei the poorest 40 per cent of teams account for 25 per cent of collective income. Of course, this comparison favours China as we are comparing distributions for aggregated units such as production teams with

Table 2:4 The Distribution of Collective Income in Hebei, 1978

Decile	Percentage of County Income	Percentage of Total Team Income
1	5.5	5.0
2	7.0	6.0
3	8.0	6.3
4	9.0	7.7
5	9.2	9.0
6	9.3	9.2
7	11.0	10.8
8	12.0	12.0
9	12.5	16.0
10	16.5	18.0

those for individual income recipients in non-socialist Third World countries. However, such data as are available to us on household incomes within a production team suggest that the intra-team distribution has remarkably underpopulated tails at both ends. For example, in Production Team No.7 of Xin Tang Brigade, Tang Tang Commune in Guangdong the standard deviation is less than one-third of the mean, and as many as 86 per cent of the 133 members of the team display an average per capita household collective income within the $(\bar{x} \pm \sigma)$ range. Bearing this in mind, there can be no doubt that the distribution of income in rural China is far more equal than in the majority of countries in Asia, Africa and Latin America. A quick comparison also suggests that the income share of the bottom 40 per cent and the top 20 per cent are not noticeably different from those displayed by the East European socialist countries.

A Lorenz curve of the distribution of collective income among production teams is depicted in Figure 2:1. The high degree of equality, as indicated by the closeness of the curve to the diagonal or line of perfect equality, is clearly visible. Even so, as mentioned earlier, our data probably understate the degree of equality in the distribution of consumption. The reasons for this are that the probable equalizing effects of income from private sector activities and remittances from urban areas are excluded. Even after all relevant adjustments were made, however, some inequality obviously would remain and it is to the causes of this remaining inequality that we now turn.

The Distribution of Income among Communes

The People's Commune is the highest form of cooperative organization in rural China and it is natural to begin an analysis of the structure of inequality by examining differences between one commune and another. In fact, intercommune inequality tends to be rather low. This is illustrated in Table 2:5 where we provide data on per capita distributed collective income for all the communes

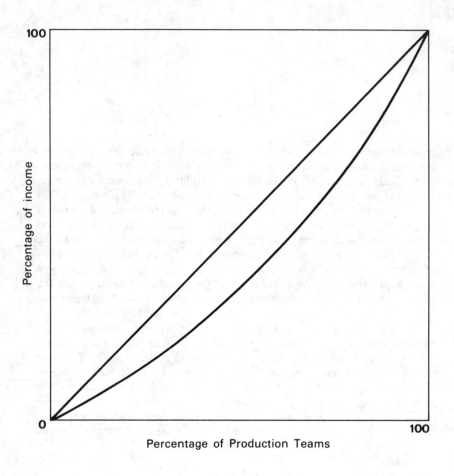

Figure 2:1

Table 2:5 Inter-commune Income Distribution: Comparisons of Three Counties
in South and Central China, 1978
(Per Capita Distributed Collective Income in Yuan Per Year)

Rank of Commune	Jia Ding County Shanghai Municipality	Shanghai County Shanghai Municipality	Fo Gang County Guangdong Province
1	294.77	309.03	92.00
2	267.99	308.47	91.70
3	256.65	273.64	86.00
4	247.76	258.68	85.00
5	246.90	256.52	85.00
6	244.22	255.55	84.00
7	243.20	253.32	82.00
8	242.25	249.16	80.00
9	241.27	246.05	76.80
10	239.28	245.97	74.00
11	238.51	242.23	72.60
12	238.42	241.19	62.00
13	238.20	240.47	
14	234.74	237.44	
15	233.10	235.07	
16	232.06	228.35	
17	228.43	227.26	
18	224.56	221.15	
19	214.61		
Mean	242.47	251.64	80.93
Range	80.16	87.88	30.00
High/Low	1.37	1.40	1.40
Standard Deviation	16.62	23.61	8.54
Coefficient of Variation	0.07	0.09	0.11

in three different counties. Two of these counties are in the Shanghai Municipality and contain exceptionally rich communes. The other is in Guangdong and
contains much poorer communes. Indeed the poorest of our communes in the
Shanghai Municipality has a per capita income that is 134 per cent higher than
the richest of our communes in Fo Gang county, Guangdong.

Jai Ding county has 19 communes with a mean income of 242.47 yuan
and a median income of 239.28 yuan. The richest commune is only 37 per cent
richer than the poorest and this is reflected in an unusually low coefficient of
variation of 0.07. The situation is very similar in Shanghai county. The mean
income is only slightly higher than the median, the ratio of the highest to the
lowest income is very modest and the coefficient of variation is low. These two

counties in the Shanghai Municipality are uniformly prosperous. Approximately 90 per cent of the land is irrigated and three crops normally are obtained each year on a unit of land, two crops of rice and one of wheat. In addition, these communes also grow cotton, rape seed, onions, melons, peas and small quantities of many other vegetables and fruit. Furthermore, industry is highly developed, the communes having many sub-contracts from state owned factories in Shanghai. Examples of commune level enterprises from Cheng Dong Commune include a towel manufacturing firm, a company making parts for light bulbs, another producing lemon extract for export, an agricultural machinery repair workshop, a bamboo ware workshop, a plastics workshop, and a firm which makes spokes for bicycles; there is also a construction team employing 400 persons, a waterway transportation team and a tractor station.

The situation is very different for the 12 communes of Fo Gang county. Far removed from the Pearl River delta which makes the hinterland around Canton so prosperous, Fo Gang suffers from both relatively poor agricultural conditions and a lack of industry. Part of the county consists of uplands where farming is difficult and the rest is plains, only a portion of which is irrigated. Main crops are rice, wheat, cassava, and beans. Industrial and sideline enterprises are not well developed and in Tang Tang Commune, which we visited, they included little more than an agricultural machinery repair shop, an orchard and forest team, a pottery workshop, one building and one boat transportation team, a pig farm and a small but impressive electricity power station.

In essentially agricultural counties such as Fo Gang, differences in per capita income between one commune and another are likely to be due to differences in the quantity and quality of land per head. These differences, in turn, often will be an inheritance of the revolution and the post-liberation land reforms of the 1950s. That is, at the level of the commune, one important component of inequality is largely structural, a historical accident arising from the way land was distributed and later consolidated into various types of collective and cooperative institutions. An implication of this view is that so long as the present distribution of land among communes exists, some inequality can be expected to be generated.

One way of testing our hypothesis of the structural determinants of inequality is to see whether there is a statistical association between the amount of land per head and per capita income. We have done this for the 12 communes of Fo Gang county, regressing 1978 per capita collective distributed income expressed in yuan (Ypc) on cultivated mou per head (L/N). The results are as follows:

$$Ypc = 47.4 + 38.95 \ (L/N)^*; \ \bar{R}^2 = 0.44$$
$$(\ 3.13)$$

where in this and the following equation

* = significant at the 1% level;

** = significant at the 10% level; and the figures in brackets are t-statistics.

In statistical terms the equation performs well. The coefficient of the independent variable is highly significant and the overall fit of the equation to the data is good. About 44 per cent of the variation in per capita income among communes in Fo Gang can be explained by variations in the amount of land per head.

A more sophisticated test of our hypothesis should incorporate not only differences in the quantity of land but also differences in the quality of land. We have indicated already that Fo Gang contains three distinct types of terrain — uplands, irrigated fields and rainfed plains — and differences in the proportions in which these three types of terrain are combined should account for at least part of the variation in per capita income.

Unfortunately, our data did not permit us to classify land into the three types. The best we could do was to separate rice land from the rest and then use the amount of land planted to rice as a proxy for the extent of irrigation. Admittedly, this is a rather crude device, but it does enable us to make some allowance for variations in land quality. We recalculated the above equation after including as an additional variable rice area as a percentage of the total cultivated area (R/L). The results are as follows:

$$Ypc = -14.7 + 37.93 \ (L/N)^* + 0.74 \ (R/L)^{**}; \ \overline{R}^2 = 0.52$$
$$(\ 3.27) \qquad \qquad (1.60)$$

The equation, once again, is rather good. The coefficient on (L/N) remains highly significant while, perhaps surprisingly, the coefficient on (R/L), our proxy for irrigation, is significant at the 10 per cent level. The overall fit improves perceptibly and as a result we are able to explain just over half the variation in the per capita income of the 12 communes. These results, we believe, are important, for they demonstrate that within a county half of the inequality among communes that exists is due to the basic structural factors of the quantity and quality of land and not to passing phenomena such as the ability of management or the set of incentives used, or the differential availability of modern inputs.

three

The Anatomy of a Commune

Communes are large organizations and contain between 15,000 and 50,000 people. Each commune, however, is divided into a number of brigades, perhaps as few as six or as many as twenty. In most communes a great deal of activity occurs at brigade level, often more than at commune level. Qie Ma Commune in Hebei is a fairly typical example. In 1978, only 10.8 per cent of total income was produced at the top level of the commune; 18.8 per cent, i.e. almost twice as much, was generated at brigade level and the remaining 70.4 per cent was income produced by the teams. At Tang Tang Commune in Guangdong the percentages were 13 (commune), 13 (brigades) and 74 (teams). Cheng Dong Commune in the Shanghai Municipality is exceptional in that it is highly industrialized and produced 46.6 per cent of its income at commune level and 25.9 and 27.5 per cent, respectively, at brigade and team levels.

The brigades, thus, play a major role in the rural economy and if one wishes to understand the structure of inequality, it is necessary to examine intra-commune differences in income. Table 3:1 contains data on distributed collective income per head in three communes. Two of these, Wu Gong and Qie Ma, are in Hebei while the third, Tang Tang, is in Guangdong. The two northern communes are significantly smaller and somewhat more prosperous than the southern commune. The degree of inequality, represented very roughly as the ratio of the highest to the lowest per capita income, is almost identical in Qie Ma and Tang Tang. Wu Gong, in contrast, appears to be considerably more unequal, its richest brigade being 2.85 times more prosperous than its poorest. The richest brigade, however, is a "model brigade" and is truly exceptional. If it were eliminated from the sample, the ratio would fall to 1.92, still a higher ratio than in the other two communes but much smaller than it is at present.

27

Table 3:1 Distributed Collective Income Per Head Among Brigades in
Three Communes, 1978

Brigade	Wu Gong Commune Hebei	Qie Ma Commune Hebei	Tang Tang Commune Guangdong
1	188.00	123.00	111.00
2	127.00	104.00	106.00
3	112.80	102.00	104.00
4	98.00	100.00	101.00
5	95.00	99.00	98.00
6	84.00	92.00	97.00
7	83.00	87.80	97.00
8	72.20	86.40	95.00
9	66.50	81.00	85.00
10	66.00		82.00
11			80.00
12			77.00
13			72.00
14			72.00
15			70.00
16			69.00
17			69.00
Average brigade income per head	111.80	99.93	84.00
Ratio of highest to lowest income	2.85	1.52	1.61
Total population	16,565	19,466	32,771

The data in Table 3:1 relate to the amalgamated distributed collective income from both brigade and team levels. Our data for Cheng Dong Commune in Shanghai Municipality, however, permit us to compare the inter-brigade distributions for each level separately, though on a per worker rather than a per capita basis. The relevant data are presented in Table 3:2. The high/low ratio for each level is very similar to the aggregate ratios in Table 3:1. But interestingly, the ratio for the combined level for Cheng Dong is lower than that at either team or brigade level. This implies the absence of any significant direct association between the (distributional) performances of different brigades at the team and the brigade levels. Indeed the rank correlation coefficient between the team-level and brigade-level incomes is −0.27. This is an intrinsically interesting finding if it is remembered that nearly three-fourths of team level incomes are derived from agriculture, whereas nearly two-thirds of brigade level income is generated by industrial activities. Relative agricultural prosperity does not seem to lead automatically to relative industrial prosperity at the intra-communal level, though such an association is obvious at regional and provincial levels. However, this observation must be interpreted against the very limited range of inequality in either agricultural (team) or industrial (brigade) incomes. Further cross-sectional comparisons of intra-commune inequality will be taken up when we consider the question of inter-team income spreads. Before that, however, we must evaluate our inter-brigade evidence on the inter-temporal behaviour of relative inequality.

Table 3:2 Distributed Collective Income Per Worker at Brigade and at Team Levels in Cheng Dong Commune, Shanghai Municipality, 1978

Brigade	Team Level	Brigade Level	Both Levels
1	578	419	509
2	512	506	510
3	509	545	521
4	502	382	471
5	474	370	442
6	460	471	463
7	450	386	434
8	431	475	442
9	430	410	425
10	423	467	435
11	417	515	447
12	407	427	413
13	397	445	411
14	377	571	416
15	355	485	384
16	348	474	374
Average	440	439	439.7
Ratio of Highest to Lowest	1.66	1.54	1.39
Total Number of Workers	8797	3438	12235

Changes Over Time in the Distribution among Brigades

One of the major questions for those interested in the distribution of income in rural China is whether, within a commune, differences between brigades tend to widen or narrow over time. We shall attempt to answer this question by looking in some detail at the experience of three communes in northern China, namely, Wu Gong Commune and Qie Ma Commune in Hebei and Evergreen Commune in Beijing Municipality.

Let us first consider Wu Gong Commune. Data are presented for three years in Table 3:3, viz. for 1966, 1972 and 1978. The analysis is conducted initially for all ten brigades in the commune; we then repeat the analysis after excluding Wu Gong Brigade to see what difference is made by this "model brigade". Since the price level was virtually stationary over the period, the money income figures used also reflect changes in real income levels.

Table 3:3 The Spread of Per Capita Collective Income Among Brigades in Wu Gong Commune

	Entire Commune			Commune Minus Wu Gong Brigade		
	1966	1972	1978	1966	1972	1978
Mean income (yuan)	39.2	62.1	99.5[a]	34.1	54.3	89.6
Income range (yuan)	65.0	91.0	121.5	28.0	27.0	60.5
Ratio of highest to lowest income	4.25	3.22	2.83	2.40	1.66	1.91
Standard deviation	18.4	26.3	36.7	9.4	10.0	20.7
Coefficient of variation	0.47	0.42	0.37	0.28	0.18	0.23

[a] This figure stands for a simple mean of brigade incomes and therefore differs from the weighted mean figure presented in Table 3:1.

As one would anticipate, average income rose considerably between 1966 and 1978, and this is true whether or not the "model brigade" is excluded. In fact, average income rose slightly faster if Wu Gong Brigade is excluded. This suggests, *prima facie*, that inequality may have diminished. The range of income of course increased, but it increased proportionately less than the mean income, again suggesting a decline in inequality. This is confirmed by examining the ratio of the highest to the lowest brigade income. In the complete sample of ten brigades, the ratio falls steadily from 4.25 in 1966 to 2.83 in 1978. If Wu Gong Brigade is removed from the sample, the ratio falls from 1966 to 1972 but then rises slightly to 1978. This suggests that after 1972 some of the brigades were breaking away from the others and rapidly catching up with Wu Gong Brigade. This particular measure of inequality therefore increased. This interpretation is confirmed by the behaviour of the coefficient of variation. It falls steadily for the full sample but rises for the reduced sample between 1972 and 1978. Hence the conclusion of this analysis is that inequality in the commune as a whole obviously declined over the entire period, but if one excludes the "model brigade" there is some evidence that it increased slightly after 1972.

The next step is to consider whether the ranking of brigades remained unchanged from one period to another, i.e., whether the brigades that were poor (or rich) in 1966 also were poor (or rich) in 1972 and 1978. We have used Kendall's rank correlation coefficients throughout and have made three different types of calculations. First, we have correlated the ranking of brigade incomes per head in 1966 with those in 1972 and 1978. In Table 3:4 this is represented as RY. Second, we have correlated the ranking of brigade incomes in 1966 with the proportional increase in per capita income between that date and 1972 or 1978. This is represented by RgY. Third, we have conducted this correlation with the figures for the absolute increase in per capita incomes. These coefficients are labelled RdY. As before, the calculations have been made both for the full set of ten brigades and for the smaller set of nine brigades from which Wu Gong Brigade is excluded.

The rank correlation (RY) between the per capita distributed collective income of all ten brigades in 1966 and that in 1972 is positive (0.36) and statistically significant at the 10 per cent level. By 1978, however, RY ceased to be statistically significant. In the restricted sample of nine brigades, RY is not significant in either period. Thus there is no support for the proposition that rich brigades invariably remain rich and the poor brigades remain poor.

If the poorer brigades were to experience higher growth rates than the richer ones, inequality would tend to diminish alongside this process of catching-up. Should this have been occurring at Wu Gong Commune, our RgY coefficients should be negative. Happily for our proposition, it can be verified that every RgY in Table 3:4 has the desired negative sign and four out of the six coefficients are statistically significant at either the 2.5 or 5 per cent level. For example, the correlation between per capita income in 1966 for all ten brigades and their percentage rate of growth during $1966 - 1978$ is $- 0.56$ and significant at the 2.5 per cent level. These results provide strong evidence that incomes in the commune are tending to converge.

In order to ensure that our results were not generated by an implicit statistical bias which would automatically throw up higher growth rates for brigades with a low absolute income level, we supplemented the RgY coefficients by the RdY ones which rely on the absolute changes in the income levels between the relevant benchmark years. It turns out that the correlation between the level of income in 1966 and the absolute increase in income over the period $1966 - 72$ (RdY_{01}) is inverse and, for the restricted sample, statistically significant at the 5 per cent level. That is, considering the entire commune minus Wu Gong Brigade, it appears that between 1966 and 1972, the lower the average income of the brigade, the higher the absolute increase in income! Clearly, there was a strong tendency for incomes to become more equal during that period. In no other period were the RdY correlations significant, however.

The Wu Gong evidence, therefore, provides extremely strong support for the proposition that initial inequalities did not lead to cumulatively divergent paths for rich and poor brigades, and fairly strong corroboration of the proposition that the poorer brigades were actually closing in on the richer ones over the period.

Table 3:4 Rank Correlations of Per Capita Income in Wu Gong Commune

		1972			1978				
		RY	RdY_{01}	RgY_{01}	RY	RdY_{02}	RgY_{02}	RdY_{12}	RgY_{12}
Entire Commune	1966	0.36^c	−0.16	$−0.42^b$	0.20	0.05	$−0.56^a$	—	—
	1972	—	—	—	0.49^a	—	—	0.18	−0.18
Nine Brigades Only	1966	0.20	$−0.44^b$	$−0.50^b$	0.00	−0.20	$−0.56^a$	—	—
	1972	—	—	—	0.37^c	—	—	0.03	−0.14

Notes: Subscripts 0, 1, 2 refer to 1966, 1972 and 1978, respectively;
[a] significant at 2.5%;
[b] significant at 5%;
[c] significant at 10%.

Table 3:5 The Spread of Per Capita Income in Qie Ma Commune

| | Nine Brigades | | Eight Brigades | |
	1970	1978	1970	1978
Mean Income (yuan)	77.9	97.3	76.2	99.3
Income Range (yuan)	46.7	42.0	46.7	36.6
Ratio of highest to lowest income	1.84	1.52	1.84	1.42
Standard deviation	15.4	12.5	15.5	11.6
Coefficient of variation	0.20	0.13	0.20	0.12

Note: In one case a brigade experienced an absolute fall in income between 1970 and 1978 and hence the calculations were repeated after dropping that brigade.

This conclusion can be checked by examining the situation of another commune in a northern wheat growing area, Qie Ma Commune. The data in Table 3:5 cover two years, 1970 and 1978. The analysis is conducted for all nine brigades and then repeated after excluding a brigade which untypically suffered an absolute fall in income over the period. As can be seen, however, the conclusions are not affected significantly by dropping the brigade that encountered severe economic difficulties, and so we will comment only on the results based on the full sample.

Average income in Qie Ma rose nearly 25 per cent in eight years. During that period the range of incomes contracted absolutely, indicating a tendency for incomes to converge. This is supported by the fact that the ratio of the highest to the lowest brigade income also fell. Finally, the coefficient of variation declined as well. Thus all the evidence in the Table indicates that intra-commune inequality declined rapidly in the 1970s.

Table 3:6 Rank Correlations of Per Capita Income in
Qie Ma Commune, 1970 – 78

	RY	RdY	RgY
Nine Brigades	0.44[b]	− 0.83[a]	− 0.83[a]
Eight Brigades	0.79[a]	0.86[a]	− 0.86[a]

Turning to Table 3:6, it can be seen that the ranking of the incomes of the nine (or eight) brigades in 1978 was positively and statistically significantly correlated with the ranking in 1970. The rate of growth of per capita income, however, was strongly and inversely correlated with the level of income in 1970. Moreover, the negative correlation was highly significant in a statistical sense. In other words, there was a marked tendency for the relatively poorer brigades of Qie Ma to grow more rapidly during 1970 – 78 than the richer brigades. Indeed this tendency was so strong that even the absolute increase in per capita income was inversely associated with the initial level of income: for all nine brigades RdY = -0.83. The evidence from Qie Ma, thus, is very similar to — indeed stronger than — that from Wu Gong: the average incomes of the brigades have shown a marked tendency to become more equal.

Finally, let us consider the case of Evergreen People's Commune. The commune is exceptional in several ways and hence one must be careful in generalizing from its experience. It is advantageously located in the Beijing Municipality. It is unusually prosperous; its per capita distributed collective income of 276 yuan a year in 1978 compares favourably with the top communes in the Shanghai Municipality. (See Table 2:5.) Moreover, it offers a wide range of universal and free social services: education to middle school level; medical services, including its own hospital; kindergartens and nurseries; 56 days of maternity leave on full pay; pensions on approximately half pay at age 60 for women and 65 for men. Few communes in China can offer such a variety of services at such high standards. At present Evergreen is one of only 60 communes in the entire country where the unit-of-account is the commune itself. For the period 1961 – 1976, however, Evergreen followed brigade-level accounting. The commune's vigorous industrial sector, accounting for 60 per cent of the commune's income, generates profits which can readily be used to further the commune's objectives, be they the achievement of a rapid rate of accumulation, or a more equal distribution, or a higher average level of consumption. Towards the end of the period, grants were frequently made to the poorer brigades in order to equalize incomes.

The commune also runs a bonus system to reward and penalize units which exceed or fall short of their production targets. Teams which exceed their quota receive a bonus of 55 per cent of the excess production, while those which underfulfill their quota receive a penalty of 30 per cent of the shortfall. In principle, this system could enable the commune leadership both to provide strong incentives to increase output and to redistribute income on the margin to the poorer brigades, should these have been set a relatively easy quota to achieve. That is, by setting difficult targets for the prosperous brigades and less difficult ones for the relatively backward ones, incentives can be provided to the latter to catch up.

Whatever the mechanisms at work, the fact is that the ranking of incomes among the 12 brigades of Evergreen People's Commune altered perceptively throughout the 1960s and then tended to revert a bit to the previous pattern during the period 1974 – 76. This is demonstrated in Table 3:7.

The table contains a complete matrix of Kendall's rank correlation coefficients for the 16-year period beginning in 1961. Thus it is possible to compare the brigade's ranking of per capita collective distributed income between any two years. The long run evolution of the distribution of income can best be seen by glancing down the column on the extreme left of the table that has been outlined in black. In this column one can compare the ranking of incomes in 1961 with every subsequent year until 1976. At the beginning of the period the correlation coefficients are fairly high and statistically significant, falling gradually to 0.52 in 1967. In the next few years, however, the coefficients fall

Table 3:7 Per Capita Income Ranks of 12 Brigades of Evergreen People's Commune, Beijing Municipality: 1961 – 1976

	1961	1962	1963	1964	1965	1966	1967	1968	1969	1970	1971	1972	1973	1974	1975	1976
1961	1.0															
1962	0.61ᵃ	1.0														
1963	.55ᵃ	.58ᵃ	1.0													
1964	.47ᵇ	.56ᵃ	.63ᵃ	1.0												
1965	.52ᵃ	.55ᵃ	.54ᵃ	.72ᵃ	1.0											
1966	.53ᵃ	.69ᵃ	.56ᵃ	.55ᵃ	.75ᵃ	1.0										
1967	.52ᵃ	.79ᵃ	.67ᵃ	.60ᵃ	.64ᵃ	.72ᵃ	1.0									
1968	.21	.36ᶜ	.55ᵃ	.66ᵃ	.64ᵃ	.50ᵇ	.52ᵃ	1.0								
1969	.12	.33ᵈ	.39ᶜ	.53ᵃ	.48ᵇ	.60ᵃ	.48ᵇ	.55ᵃ	1.0							
1970	.18	.33ᵈ	.39ᶜ	.47ᵇ	.48ᵇ	.56ᵃ	.48ᵇ	.48ᵇ	.70ᵃ	1.0						
1971	.20	.35ᵈ	.47ᵇ	.43ᶜ	.35ᵈ	.43ᶜ	.47ᵇ	.41ᶜ	.69ᵃ	.69ᵃ	1.0					
1972	.14	.05	.35ᶜ	.40ᶜ	.14	.09	.08	.26	.29ᵈ	.17	.31ᵈ	1.0				
1973	.17	.08	.32ᵈ	.34ᵃ	.23	.09	.11	.17	.32ᵈ	.20	.40ᶜ	.58ᵃ	1.0			
1974	.42ᶜ	.15	.39ᶜ	.32	.24	.17	.18	.12	.15	.10	.17	.53ᵃ	.69ᵃ	1.0		
1975	.42ᶜ	.15	.52ᵃ	.38ᵃ	.30	.17	.24	.24	.15	.09	.17	.53ᵃ	.63ᵃ	.88ᵃ	1.0	
1976	.32ᵈ	.17	.41ᶜ	.34ᵈ	.20	.09	.20	.14	.10	.11	.18	.65ᵃ	.62ᵃ	.81ᵃ	.84ᵃ	1.0
Mean	162.3	176.5	158.0	145.	156.7	157.3	163.3	134.3	126.6	150.1	155.4	153.4	167.9	175.3	177.9	193.3
Range	110.0	81.0	121.0	68.0	88.0	101.0	89.0	73.0	72.0	57.0	57.0	104.0	86.0	82.0	62.0	76.0
Highest/Lowest	2.02	1.62	2.22	1.59	1.72	1.83	1.73	1.67	1.82	1.46	1.49	2.18	1.74	1.65	1.43	1.51
Standard Deviation	29.8	23.4	29.2	17.9	23.7	27.0	27.5	22.3	21.9	18.7	19.9	30.7	25.4	24.5	19.9	19.3
Coefficient of Variation	0.18	0.13	0.18	0.12	0.15	0.17	0.17	0.17	0.17	0.12	0.13	0.20	0.15	0.14	0.11	0.10

Notes: 1. All figures are Kendall's rank correlation coefficients.
2. Significance levels: a = 1%; b = 2.5%; c = 5.0%; d = 10.0%.

dramatically and are not statistically different from zero. The lowest point is reached in 1972 with a coefficient of 0.14.

Thereafter the correlation coefficients rise again and become statistically significant in 1974 onwards. That is, the rankings of per capita income in 1974 – 76 are positively correlated with those in 1961, suggesting that the previous ranking had partially reasserted itself. Another way of expressing this is to say that after 1972 the ranking of brigade income became much more stable. This can be seen in the triangular set of high and significant coefficients in the lower right hand corner of the table. Note, however, that the coefficient of variation fell steadily after 1972 and the ratio of the highest to lowest brigade income reached its lowest point in 1975, rising slightly again in 1976. Thus the data suggest that especially in the middle of the 1960s there was no tendency for the rich brigades to remain rich and the poor to remain poor: the rank correlations were low. In the 1970s, the rankings became more stable, but within the rankings inequality (as measured by the range of incomes, the ratio of highest to lowest income and the coefficient of variation) diminished considerably.

The evidence from all three communes, hence, is consistent. No tendency can be detected for the intra-commune distribution of income to become worse over time. On the contrary, much of the evidence points in the opposite direction. In the two cases where we were able to measure it, the growth of per capita income was inversely associated with the initial level of income, and in all three cases the dispersion of incomes around the average was lower in the 1970s than in the 1960s.

These findings must be qualified. It is quite possible that inequality within the village or the commune has declined gradually over time, yet these changes may have been offset, or even more than offset, by an unequal pattern of agricultural growth which has resulted in greatly increased regional inequality. That is, reduced inequality within a particular locality may have been accompanied by greater inequality in the rural areas as a whole. This in no way detracts from the achievements at the local level, which appear from our investigations to have been remarkable, but it does not follow from these results that interprovincial inequality also is declining.

Equalizing Factors

There are a great many devices that have been used in China to ensure that inequality does not become unacceptably great. County authorities may provide technical assistance to communes suffering from unsatisfactory management. They may make capital grants to relatively poor communes — and through them, or sometimes even directly to poor brigades — or they may provide loans that either are free of interest or carry a low interest charge. Equally, the county may give priority to poor communes in the allocation of scarce modern inputs. In Fo Gang county, for example, the average allocation of fertilizer was 45 jin[1] per mou, yet in 1978 eight poor brigades were allocated an extra

---

[1]   1 jin = ½ kilogramme.

40 jin per mou in order to help them increase grain yields and income.

Similar policies can be applied within the commune. Grants to the weaker production teams and brigades from the profits of commune level enterprises are not uncommon. In Tang Tang Commune, for instance, as much as 41.6 per cent of the profits were distributed in this way in 1977. Sometimes labour is provided to teams which lack labour in order to undertake specific investment projects, e.g., land drainage. Alternatively, interest free or low interest loans may be provided for agreed investments, e.g. in flood control. Finally, weaker teams may be given preferential use of tractors and other equipment owned by the brigade.

One of the most powerful factors tending to equalize incomes among brigades is grants and loans for capital accumulation. This is illustrated in Table 3:8 for Wu Gong Commune, where the average for the three richest brigades is compared with the average for the three poorest brigades.

The differences in distributed collective income per capita (line 1) and distributed collective income per workday (line 2) are more than 100 per cent between the top and bottom three brigades. A similar difference is observed in net income per workday (line 3), where net income equals collective distributed income plus the contributions made to the welfare and accumulation funds. Net income, thus, is equivalent to value added, and line 3 is a measure of the productivity of labour unadjusted for variations in fixed assets per workday.

One reason why the top brigades enjoy high labour productivity and incomes is because they have a relatively high ratio of capital to labour. This is indicated in line 4: fixed assets per workday are 2.47 times greater on the top three brigades than on the bottom three. Similarly, variable material costs per workday (line 5) are three times higher on the rich brigades than on the poor. That is, workers on the rich brigades have considerably more inputs with which to work. As a result, their incomes are higher.

Grants and loans, however, can be channelled to the poor brigades to enable them to increase their fixed assets, raise their capital-labour ratio and thereby increase the productivity of their labour and their income per head. In fact, this is precisely what is done. Whether expressed as a percentage of net income (line 7) or of fixed assets (line 8), the poorest three brigades in Wu Gong receive more than five times more grants and loans than the richest three brigades. This, clearly, is a vigorous application in a socialist context of a policy of redistribution with growth. Given time, such capital transfers in favour of the poor are bound to reduce inequality considerably.[2]

---

2   The data in Table 3:8 enable us to make a very crude estimate of the proportionate rate of accumulation in the two groups of brigades. Let us ignore contributions to the welfare fund and assume that the figures in line 3 minus line 2 = accumulation per workday from own savings = A. Line 3 times line 7 = accumulation per workday from grants and loans = B. Total accumulation per workday = A + B = C. The rate of accumulation = C divided by line 4. It turns out that for the three richest brigades 0.25 yuan is invested for each yuan of fixed assets, whereas for the three poorest brigades the estimate is 0.5 yuan. The results overstate the two magnitudes partly because of our exclusion of public welfare funds, and partly because some grants and loans might have gone into financing working capital, i.e., production cost outlays, rather than into fixed asset accumulation exclusively. Nevertheless, the exercise provides an arithmetical illustration of the argument in the text.

Table 3:8 Income and Production Indicators on Wu Gong Commune, 1978

		Richest Three Brigades	Poorest Three Brigades
1.	Distributed income per capita (yuan per annum)	143.00	68.00
2.	Distributed income per workday (yuan)	0.78	0.36
3.	Net income per workday (yuan)	1.21	0.56
4.	Fixed assets per workday (yuan)	2.10	0.85
5.	Production costs per workday (yuan)	1.59	0.53
6.	Ratio of net income to production costs	0.83	1.30
7.	Grants and loans as a percentage of net income	7.96	40.37
8.	Grants and loans as a percentage of fixed assets	4.80	26.26

There is a second powerful force tending to reduce inequality among brigades, namely, diminishing returns to the use of material inputs. It can be seen in line 6 of Table 3:8 that net income as a ratio of production costs is much lower on the rich brigades than on the poor. That is, the productivity of non-labour factors of production declines as one moves from poor brigades to rich, or from brigades where material inputs are scarce to those where they are relatively abundant. The implication of this is that on the margin an additional dose of, say, fertilizer raises output and incomes relatively more on a brigade with a relatively low level of application of fertilizer.

This is an important empirical finding that will be examined in detail in Part Two. A preliminary investigation, however, can be conducted here.

In Table 3:9 we examine the relationship between net income (or value added) and the material costs of production for all ten brigades of Wu Gong Commune in 1978. In a sense Table 3:9 contains a detailed examination of line 6 of Table 3:8. Output in the commune is divided into agricultural production and so-called sideline activities, and regression equations are estimated for both of these sectors separately as well as for aggregate output. Furthermore, logarithmic as well as non-logarithmic forms of the explanatory variable are used. In all cases the dependent variable is the productivity of material inputs in the sector, i.e., the ratio of net income to production costs (NY/PC), specified in either its logarithmic or non-logarithmic form.

The independent variable in the case of sideline activities is production cost (PC) divided by the number of workdays (D), that is, the variable capital-to-labour ratio (PC/D). The same independent variable is used in the equations concerned with aggregate output. When examining agricultural production,

Table 3:9 The Productivity of Material Inputs in Wu Gong Commune, 1978

Equation Number	Activity	Dependent Variable	Constant	Explanatory Variables				$\overline{R}^2$
				(PC/L)	log(PC/L)	(PC/D)	log(PC/D)	
1	Agricultural Production	$(NY/PC)_{ag}$	1.61	-0.67^c (2.23)				0.31
2		$(NY/PC)_{ag}$	0.90		-0.86^b (2.58)			0.39
3		$\log(NY/PC)_{ag}$	-0.23		-1.03 (2.76)			0.42
4	Sideline Activities	$(NY/PC)_s$	1.21			-0.71^c (2.20)		0.30
5		$(NY/PC)_s$	0.30				-0.45^a (3.95)	0.62
6		$\log(NY/PD)_s$	-1.01				-0.53^a (4.36)	0.67
7	Aggregate Output	(NY/PC)	1.49			-0.46^b (2.42)		0.35
8		(NY/PC)	0.92				-0.55^a (3.58)	0.57
9		$\log(NY/PC)$	-0.12				-0.48^a (4.27)	0.66

Notes: 1. Figures in parentheses are t-statistics.
2. Significance levels: a = 1%; b = 2.5%; c = 5%.

however, we use as the explanatory variable production costs per 100 mou of cropped land (PC/L).

The results are quite unambiguous. All of the explanatory variables have the expected negative sign, indicating the presence of diminishing returns, and all are statistically highly significant. The double-logarithmic equations seem to fit the data best and provide the best explanation of the forces at work. Equations 1 – 3 show that a rise in inputs per unit of land in agriculture leads to a sharp fall in the productivity of non-labour factors of production. It is natural to expect that when brigades encounter sharply diminishing returns in agriculture they will diversify their activities and begin to shift resources into manufacturing and other sideline occupations. Here, too, however, they will encounter diminishing returns rather quickly, as equations 4 – 6 indicate. That is, a rise in the capital-labour ratio in industry leads to some fall in the productivity of capital and consequently to a less than proportionate rise in the productivity of labour and in per capita income. The richer is the brigade to begin with, i.e., the higher is (PC/D), the more powerful is this effect.

When the two sectors are aggregated the phenomenon of diminishing returns remains: a rise in (PC/D) lowers (NY/PC). Equations 7 – 9 make this plain.

The results in Table 3:9 are derived from the data for the ten brigades of Wu Gong Commune for 1978. Even though the diminishing returns are evident in all sectors and all forms of the equation, it could be argued that the relationship might have been an accidental one. We have therefore conducted a second exercise in which we pool the relevant data for the 10 brigades for the 3 benchmark years for which they are available, 1966, 1972 and 1978. Since there was virtually no inflation, the use of current price yuan data does not distort the results. Consider first the scattergram in Figure 5:2, where the ratio of aggregate net income to aggregate production costs, NY/PC, is plotted on the y-axis. The x-axis measures the level of production costs per capita, PC/N, rather than per workday. The plot shows a striking non-linear relationship between NY/PC and PC/N, with the slope negative throughout, but decreasing in absolute value. The full curve, it can be seen easily, consists of three staggered segments, one for each of the benchmark years, and the negative relationship is evident in each. Unfortunately, for want of disaggregated data for 1966 and 1972, this pooled-data relationship could not be investigated for separate activities, but the strength of the aggregate relationship lends additional credence to the activity-level results presented in Table 3:9. We tested the statistical strength of the relationship in Figure 5:2. As might have been expected, the estimated coefficients have the correct signs and are highly significant, as the following estimated equation shows:

$$\log(NY/N) = \begin{array}{cc} 2.71 + & 0.45 \log(PC/N) \quad R^2 = 0.69 \\ (12.42) & (7.93) \end{array} \qquad N = 30$$

where NY/N = net income per capita in yuan
PC/N = production costs per capita in yuan.

It then follows inevitably that labour productivity will increase less rapidly than the means of production,[3] and the more capital intensive is production, the more will this be true. Hence if the richer brigades increase their capital-labour ratios at the same pace as the poorer ones, the latter will experience the faster rise in output per workday and hence, ultimately, in per capita income. Thus it is that diminishing returns in combination with capital transfers to poor brigades constitute strong forces tending to reduce inequality within the communes of rural China.

Inter-Team Inequality

Each brigade is divided into a number of teams. A team usually coincides with a neighbourhood of a village, although in small villages the team may include the entire village. The brigade, in turn, is either a cluster of small villages or, more frequently, a grouping of teams from a single village. There may be as few as two teams in a brigade or perhaps as many as 20. It is always possible, of course, that the tendency toward equality between brigades might obscure great inequality at the level of the production team. It is instructive to examine the intra-commune as well as intra-brigade profiles of the average distributed collective income of teams. This becomes possible on the basis of the data presented in Table 3:10 covering all the teams in the ten brigades of Wu Gong Commune.

Table 3:10 Distributed Collective Income among the 36 Production Teams of Wu Gong People's Commune, 1978

Brigade	Number of Teams	Per Capita Income (yuan)				
		50 – 60	60 – 80	80 – 100	100 – 150	Over 150
Wu Gong	3					3
Zou Cun	5		1		4	
Guan Zhuang	3		2		1	
Dong Song	2		2			
Yang Zhuang	4		1	1	2	
Wang Qiao	4			3	1	
Song Qiao	3	1	2			
Kao Qiao	3			1	2	
Yuan Zi	3		2			
Geng Kou	6		4	1	1	
Total	36	1	14	7	11	3

[3] This is obvious from the identity,
$$P = (NY/PC)(PC/D)$$
where P is the productivity of labour.

The first observation is the moderate level of inter-team inequality at an intra-commune level. Thirty-two of the 36, or 89 per cent of the teams have a per capita income between 60 and 150 yuan. The moderate inter-brigade inequality, discussed earlier, now reflects itself in the fact that the intra-brigade inequality between teams is similar in general for most brigades to the overall intra-commune inequality between teams.

The table also permits us to determine whether the rich brigades tend to consist of teams all of which are equally prosperous, and poor brigades of teams all of which are uniformly poor.

It will be seen that there are 36 production teams divided among ten brigades in Wu Gong Commune, of which the richest is Wu Gong Brigade with an average distributed collective income of 188 yuan a year (see Table 3:1) and the poorest is Song Qiao with only 66 yuan per year. The distribution of income among teams appears to be bimodal, although no particular significance should be attached to this. More significant is the fact that there are few exceptionally poor or exceptionally rich teams; most fall within a fairly narrow band. In a sense, of course, this is what one should expect given that the degree of inequality is so low.

There are only three teams with an average income greater than 150 yuan per annum. All three of them are in Wu Gong Brigade and, moreover, no team in Wu Gong Brigade earns less than 150 yuan. That is, one brigade in the commune has all of the rich teams and none of the poor ones. The per capita income of these three teams in 1978 was 150 yuan for Team No.2, 176 yuan for Team No.1 and 223 yuan for Team No.3. Clearly, Wu Gong Brigade's elevation as a "model" brigade is warranted by its performance.

Turning to the poorest brigade, Song Qiao, we can see that it also contains three teams. One of these is the poorest in the commune and the other two are in the next lowest income bracket. Considering Song Qiao and Wu Gong brigades in isolation, there is just a hint that the distribution of income among teams may not be random. That is, one may be tempted to conclude that there are forces at work which tend systematically to favour all the teams of some brigades relative to all the teams of other brigades. However, Wu Gong and Song Qiao are not typical, and a closer inspection of Table 3:10 shows that the existence of elements within brigades tending to equalize the incomes of teams — be they the impact of redistribution policies or of low initial inequalities — is not strong enough to squeeze all the teams of any brigade apart from Wu Gong into the same income size-class. Consider, for example, Zou Cun and Guan Zhuong brigades: both of these have teams which differ markedly from each other in terms of average incomes.

A similar picture emerges from an examination of the data in Table 3:11 on Cheng Dong People's Commune. This is a very rich commune in the Shanghai Municipality, with a large number of production teams. Average incomes not only are high, they are remarkably uniform. In fact, 95 per cent of the 141 teams in the commune have an income between 150 and 250 yuan a year. Only four teams have more than this and only three have less. Apart from Zhou Jia

Table 3:11 Distributed Collective Income Among the 141 Production Teams of Cheng Dong People's Commune, Shanghai Municipality, 1978

Brigade	Number of Teams	Per Capita Income (yuan)					
		120–130	130–150	150–180	180–200	200–250	250–300
Chang Chang	14		1	2	5	6	
Yang Jia	10				4	6	
Zhou Jia	6					5	1
Cheng Dong	7			1	1	4	1
Kao Qiao	8				3	5	
Li Xin	10				3	6	1
Cheng Qiao	8				3	5	
Xu Wang	10			2	5	3	
Wang Lou	11			1	4	6	
Liu Cun	9	2		3	1	3	
Zhang Gu	10			3	5	2	
Xiao Hong	13			4	5	4	
Wang Shi	9			1	4	4	
Dong Chen	8			2	3	2	1
Zhan Bang	8			1	3	4	
Total	141	2	1	20	49	65	4

Brigade with its one very rich team and its remaining five teams in the next lowest income bracket, there appears to be no tendency for rich teams to be grouped together in a few brigades and poor ones to be concentrated in other brigades. As closely as one can judge by inspection, the distribution of income appears to be more or less random within the 150 – 250 yuan range.

Let us now focus more closely on the magnitude and the sources of inequality between teams within a single brigade. For this purpose, we will analyse the inter-team data from the poorest brigade of all the communes that we visited. This is Xin Tang Brigade of Tang Tang People's Commune in Guangdong Province, South China. Xin Tang is the poorest of 17 brigades in its commune and in 1978 its per capita distributed collective income was only 69 yuan.[4]

The population of the brigade is 3,036. The total area is 2,276 mou, of which 1,755 mou are irrigated. The main crop is rice, followed by a bit of wheat and sweet potatoes. Mushrooms are a speciality of the brigade, and of course there are also pigs and vegetables. Sideline activities at the brigade-level are weakly developed: the brigade had a repair workshop, a brick-making unit, a forestry and orchard unit and a barber's shop. Between them, their activities

---

4 Xin Tang is brigade number 17 in Tang Tang Commune in Table 3:1, while Tang Tang Commune is commune number 6 in Fo Gang county in Table 2:5.

produced only 9 per cent of the brigade's total income; the rest was produced by the teams.

There are 19 production teams in Xin Tang Brigade with an average distributed collective income that varies between 109 and 22 yuan. Thus the ratio of the highest to the lowest income is 4.95, perhaps a surprisingly high ratio. The income of each team in the brigade is listed in descending order in Table 3:12.

Table 3:12 Distributed Collective Income Per Head among the 19 Teams of Xin Tang Brigade, Tang Tang Commune, 1978

Team	Per Capita Income
	(yuan)
1	109
2	93
3	83
4	80
5	79
6	73
7	73
8	71
9	70
10	59
11	59
12	59
13	55
14	54
15	51
16	39
17	36
18	27
19	22
Brigade Average	69
Ratio of highest to lowest income	4.95

Agricultural production is of course the main source of income for the teams. Following our earlier analysis in Chapter 2 of the distribution of per capita income among all the communes of Fo Gang county, we have tried to discover the main determinants of variations in agricultural income per capita (AGYPC). Our hypothesis, once again, is that differences in cultivated area per capita (CAPC) and in the quality of land as measured by the proportion of the cultivated area that is irrigated (IRCA) explain most of the variation. This hypothesis seems to be supported by the data as the following regression equation indicates:

$$\text{AGYPC} = -204.00^* + 127.21 \text{ CAPC}^* + 231.52 \text{ IRCA}^*;$$
$$(-2.97) \qquad (2.89) \qquad\qquad (4.00)$$
$$\bar{R}^2 = 0.51; F = 8.41; N = 19$$

where the figures in parentheses are t-statistics
and * = significant at the 1% level

As can readily be seen, the equation easily passes all the usual statistical tests and explains about 51 per cent of the variation in agricultural income per head. We also tried labour power per head of the population as an additional explanatory variable, the hypothesis being that relatively prosperous teams are those where the ratio of workers to total population is high. The variable carried the expected positive sign but the coefficient was not statistically significant.

It is possible to learn a bit more about the structure of inequality at the team level by examining the variation in several key agricultural variables. Some of the relevant information is presented in Table 3:13.

Table 3:13 Key Agricultural Variables of the 19 Teams of Xin Tang Brigade, 1978

Variable	Mean Value	Ratio of Highest to Lowest Value	Coefficient of Variation
AGYPC (yuan)	74.41	2.94	0.22
CAPC (mou)	0.65	1.63	0.12
IRCA	0.84	1.32	0.07
Population/labour force	2.44	—	0.20
Grain yield (jin/mou)	483	1.97	0.16
Main rice yield (jin/mou)	656	1.45	0.10
Distributed Income per capita	62.7[a]	4.95	0.35
Value of a Workday (yuan)	0.43	3.25	0.26

[a] This is an unweighted mean, and hence differs from the mean for the brigade in Table 3:12.

One of the things that emerges clearly from the table is that there is relatively little inequality among teams in each of the key variables determining income taken separately. Whether one looks at the coefficient of variation or at the ratio of the highest to lowest value of a variable, there is only a modest difference in land per head, the extent of irrigation, the burden of dependency or output per unit of land. This suggests that inequality is the cumulative outcome of several small differences rather than a result of a single dominant cause. In fact, variations in AGYPC account for approximately one-half of the variations in total per capita income across teams; and one-half of these variations in AGYPC are statistically explained by the variations in the per capita availability of cultivated land.

It is perhaps noteworthy that the coefficient of variation for AGYPC is lower, at 0.22, than that for distributed income per head, 0.35. Since agricultural income constitutes the major proportion of the total income available for distribution, it is likely that non-agricultural income is much more unequal between teams than is agricultural income. That is, inequality in distributed collective income may originate not in the agricultural sector but in non-agricultural activities. Before concluding that sideline activities are disequalizing, however, it is important to look behind the per capita income figures reported in Table 3:12.

The Equalizing Effects of Outside Employment

The richest team in the brigade (Team No.1) has a diversified economy. In addition to the usual grains, in their case grown almost entirely under irrigation, the team produces fungus spores for medicinal purposes, mushrooms and vegetables. It also has a construction group that works both inside and outside the team. When the construction group works outside the team they are allowed to retain 20 per cent of their earnings and in addition receive 10 workpoints for every 1.60 yuan that goes to the team. For work inside the team, members receive 10 workpoints per day. Nearly 15 per cent of the total income of the team is generated by the construction group alone.

Team No.19 would appear to be the poorest. Its population of 80 persons is large in proportion to its land area of only 39 mou. Rather than try to eke out a living on less than 0.5 mou per head, however, many members of the labour force have obtained employment outside the team, typically in county owned factories. Specifically, of the 18 households in the team, 12 have at least one member working outside the team; of the 36 members of the labour force, 14 are working outside the team. That is, 38.9 per cent of the team's labour force is occupied outside the team, as compared to 22.2 per cent for the brigade as a whole. The average earnings of an outside worker are approximately 45 yuan per month, of which approximately 15 yuan per month are sent back to the parent teams by way of private remittances. A quick calculation can demonstrate how such an income source can alter the relative position of "rich" and "poor" teams. Using brigade aggregates, it turns out that the overall average distributed collective income per capita of 64 yuan is supplemented by 17 yuan from remittances, i.e., by 26.6 per cent; the poorest team's average of 22 yuan is augmented to the tune of 32 yuan, or by 145.5 per cent; the corresponding figures for Team No.2 (which has the same size as the poorest team) which has an average of 93 yuan are 11 yuan, or 11.8 per cent. Hence, Table 3:12 can be seriously misleading unless it is interpreted alongside data for supplementary income sources. It is interesting that according to the consensus of the officials of the Brigade, it was the team ranking a joint 10th by the distributed collective income per capita criterion that was the poorest after supplementary income had been incorporated into the comparison.

Fortunately, our data do permit us to make an approximate comparison after including the effects of outside employment. Outside employment could be of two types: firstly, team members could be employed at the collective level within the brigade. Such employment, the figures for which are given in Table 3:14, is recorded on the basis of the value of the workday at brigade level. This figure is 0.8 yuan, which is 23 per cent higher than the team-workday value for the richest team, 86 per cent higher than the average team-level value of 0.43 yuan, and four times that for the poorest team. Since the wages of collective level workers are in the main paid to the teams from which the workers come, such employment is lucrative for the team. In virtually all the communes we visited, it was a general policy to draw workers from teams for collective employment in proportion to the team's share in the total labour force. This policy is clearly redistributive in favour of the poorer teams.

However, despite the intention of the policy, it can be confirmed that the share of some teams in collective employment is more than twice that of some others. However, it can also be seen that this share is not positively or negatively related to the income level of teams, which invited the conclusion that such employment would, on average, still be redistributive. Since the figures for distributed collective income already include the wages from team workers employed at brigade or commune levels, we have calculated the profile of team incomes per capita on the assumption that none of them had any workers employed at collective level. In one variant, we assume that such workers have a zero marginal product upon their return to their teams; the resultant income profile is labelled YA in Table 3·14. In the second variant these workers are assumed to have a marginal product equal to the observed distributed collective income per capita; this income variable is called YB. We then calculate a third variable YC which stands for the distributed collective income per capita plus the per capita level of remittances from workers employed outside the commune altogether. The results are interesting, and tend to corroborate the equalization proposition. Without either form of non-team-level employment, the mean income per capita, YA, is 54.3, with a coefficient of variation of 0.39, and a high/low ratio of 6.76. Including collective, i.e. brigade and commune level employment, the mean rises to 62.7, while the coefficient of variation and the high/low ratio drop to 0.35 and 4.95 respectively. Once outside employment is included as well, YC displays corresponding figures of 79.8, 0.29 and 3.25. Clearly, outside employment has an equalizing effect on inter-team inequality.

Some Aspects of Inequality among Households

Team No.12 of Xin Tang Brigade in Tang Tang Commune had a population of 143 in 1979 grouped into 30 households (in 1978 there were 28 households). It had 56 workers engaged in agriculture who cultivated 103 mou of land, of which 78 mou were irrigated. In addition, there were eight other workers, or

Table 3:14 The Equalizing Effects of Outside Employment on Team Incomes in Xin Tang Brigade, 1978

Team Number	Labour Force as a % of Population	% of Labour Force Employed in Collective Industry	Outside Employment as % of Labour Force	Team Level Value of Labour Day (yuan)	Distributed Collective Income per Capita (yuan)	Alternative Income Measures		
						YA (yuan)	YB (yuan)	YC (yuan)
1	37.80	12.77	36.88	0.65	109	99.3	104.6	134.1
2	56.10	8.70	10.87	0.55	93	83.2	87.8	104.0
3	47.95	7.14	7.14	0.50	83	76.2	79.0	89.2
4	40.43	8.77	20.17	0.41	80	72.9	75.7	94.7
5	39.61	8.54	19.51	0.62	79	72.2	74.9	92.9
6	42.06	15.55	42.22	0.48	73	59.9	64.7	105.0
7	44.00	7.57	28.79	0.50	73	66.3	68.8	95.8
8	55.40	10.17	17.80	0.44	71	59.7	63.7	88.7
9	47.79	7.56	28.57	0.46	70	62.8	65.3	94.6
10	45.76	6.62	17.22	0.42	59	52.9	54.7	73.2
11	44.32	7.69	23.08	0.35	59	52.2	54.2	77.4
12	48.94	10.14	7.25	0.40	59	49.1	52.0	65.4
13	41.28	14.45	12.22	0.43	55	43.1	46.4	64.1
14	42.11	12.50	27.50	0.40	54	43.5	46.3	74.8
15	41.79	7.14	17.86	0.36	51	45.0	46.6	64.4
16	29.60	13.34	29.56	0.36	39	31.1	32.6	48.5
17	32.84	9.09	31.81	0.30	36	30.0	31.1	54.8
18	41.73	11.32	18.87	0.30	27	17.6	18.8	41.2
19	26.83	13.64	63.63	0.20	22	14.7	15.5	52.7
Mean	42.44	10.14	24.26	0.43	62.7	54.3	57.0	79.8
Highest/Lowest	2.09	2.35	8.91	3.25	4.95	6.76	6.75	3.25
Coefficient of Variation	0.17	0.27	0.54	0.24	0.35	0.39	0.40	0.29

12.5 per cent of the labour force, engaged in outside activities. The total net income of the team in 1978 was 14,263 yuan, of which 10,946 yuan originated in agriculture and 3,317 yuan was generated in sideline and other activities. These totals, of course, are greater than distributed income because they include contributions to the welfare fund and to the fund for collective accumulation.

Furthermore, each household engaged in private production. The private plots were of a uniform size equal to 0.05 mou per head. Households also raised six or seven ducks, geese or chickens and an average of 1.4 pigs.

The characteristics of 27 of the 28 households in Team No.12 in 1978 are described in Table 3:15.

Table 3:15 Characteristics of 27 Households of Production Team No.12, Xin Tang Brigade, Tang Tang Commune, 1978

Variable	Mean Value	Coefficient of Variation	Ratio of Highest to Lowest Value
Number of persons per household (HH)	4.82	0.44	8.00
Number of workers per household (LF)	2.04	0.48	4.00
HH/LF	2.59	0.51	6.00
Total income in yuan of household (TY)	324.6	0.44	7.18
Income in yuan from workpoints (WPY)	285.5	0.50	7.13
Other income in yuan (OY)	39.9	1.38	(min = 0; max = 197.7)
TY/HH (yuan)	71.6	0.33	3.81
WPY/HH (yuan)	64.8	0.43	6.02
OY/HH (yuan)	6.9	1.34	(min = 0; max = 32.9)
TY/LF (yuan)	165.8	0.36	4.42
WPY/LF (yuan)	139.6	0.27	2.84
OY/LF (yuan)	26.7	1.76	(min = 0; max = 197.7)

As one can see, there was considerable variation in most of the variables across households. The smallest family was a single person household while the largest contained eight persons. We interviewed the largest family and it may be of interest to see the sources of their income and its size:

Total distributed collective income   410.00 yuan
Total private income, of which   275.11 yuan

net income from pig breeding	154.00
net income from peanuts	16.11
net income from vegetables	50.00
net income from potatoes	22.40
net income from ducks and geese	32.60
Total income from all sources	685.11 yuan
Average income per head from all sources	85.64 yuan

The noteworthy thing about this exceptionally large household is that 40.2 per cent of its total income originated from private sector economic activities. Even so, income per head was modest and consequently little was saved for future contingencies: our estimate of the household's rate of saving was 1.8 per cent.

A prosperous family of average size that we interviewed contained four persons. Their income account was as follows:

Total distributed collective income		263.00 yuan
Total private sector income, of which		231.76 yuan
net income from two pigs	164.00	
net income from two geese	6.12	
net income from peanuts	6.14	
net income from sweet potatoes	10.50	
net income from vegetables	45.00	
Total income from all sources		494.76 yuan
Income per head from all sources		123.64 yuan

Average income clearly was much higher. More surprising, income from the private sector was nearly half the total, viz. 46.6 per cent. The savings rate, at 9.1 per cent of total income, also was impressive. This is especially true when one remembers that these household savings are additional to the substantial collective savings already realised before distribution at team, brigade and commune levels.

These sketches of particular households give one an impression of the types of situations that are encountered, but they are not a substitute for a systematic analysis. We have data on 27 of the 28 households from this poorest team and we can use this data to demonstrate the importance of demographic phenomena in determining the distribution of income among households of a team.

The most important source of income to a family is workpoints obtained from collective activities. Therefore we have made money workpoints per household (WPY/HH) our dependent variable and regressed this on the number of dependents in the household divided by its labour force (DEP/LF) — a measure of dependency — and the number of workpoints earned by each member of the household's labour force (WPY/LF). The results of the regression were as follows:

$$WPY/HH = 53.68 - 19.49 \text{ (DEP/LF)} + 0.30 \text{ (WPY/LF)}; \overline{R}^2 = 0.73$$
$$ (8.47) \phantom{\text{(DEP/LF)} +} (3.69) \phantom{\text{(WPY/LF)};} F = 36.3$$

That is, workpoint income per capita is significantly directly related to the earning capacity of the workers of the household (WPY/LF), and strongly and inv ely associated with the number of dependents each worker must support. In .her words, the higher the dependency ratio the lower is collective income per head. This implies that families with a relatively high proportion of infants or of elderly persons would suffer from low per capita income from the collective sector. Everything else being equal, one would expect them to be at a considerable disadvantage and to experience relative poverty.

Fortunately, everything else is not equal. Families with low incomes from workpoints compensate for this by increasing their "other income", presumably from employment outside the team and from irregular activities not rewarded in terms of workpoints. That is, other income (OY) appears to be positively associated with the number of dependents per member of the labour force (DEP/LF) and negatively associated with money workpoints per member of the labour force (WPY/LF). The regression equation for our 27 families is as follows:

$$OY/HH = 7.73 + 5.94 \text{ (DEP/LF)} - 0.074 \text{ (WPY/LF)}; \overline{R}^2 = 0.61$$
$$ (6.57) \phantom{\text{(DEP/LF)} -} (2.29) \phantom{\text{(WPY/LF)};} F = 21.6$$

The direction of the association of WPY/HH and OY/HH with the common set of explanatory variables runs in opposite directions. This would be consistent with OY/HH playing a compensatory role to the low levels of WPY/HH associated with a labour shortage at the household level. Not surprisingly, WPY/HH and OY/IIH are significantly negatively related, the simple correlation coefficient being -0.62.

These results suggest that "other income" is an equalizing factor across households. Demographic forces may lead to inequality in the distribution of collective income, but opportunities outside the commune and in the private economy offset this, at least in part, and reduce inequality considerably below what it otherwise would have been. Thus Table 3:15 shows an average workpoint income per household member of 64.8 yuan, with a coefficient of variation of 0.43 and a highest/lowest ratio of 6.02. When other income is totted up as well, the total income per household member rises on average to 71.6 yuan, while the coefficient of variation and the highest/lowest ratio drop to 0.33 and 3.81 respectively. There is undoubtedly a complex trade-off between private and collective sector activities. The pitfalls in making any generalizations on the basis of our results are too obvious to be emphasized, but our analysis suggests an interesting paradox: private sector economic activities may have led to a reduction of inequalities generated in the collective sector!

PART TWO

*EQUALIZING GROWTH IN THE
CHINESE COMMUNE*

four

Equalizing Growth: An Introduction

In Part Two of this monograph, we attempt to develop a simple numerical model which is designed to investigate the process of growth within a commune. That is, we explore the internal dynamics of a commune in an effort to discover whether over time economic growth tends to accentuate or diminish the degree of income inequality at the local level. We are not concerned to construct an abstract model as such but to provide a conceptual framework that will enable us to make sense of a commune's observable growth process. The model is based on statistical evidence collected in two communes, namely, the predominantly agricultural Wu Gong Commune in Hebei Province and the highly industrialized Cheng Dong Commune in Jia Ding County in the Shanghai Municipality. All of the evidence we have used was obtained during the course of a field trip conducted in June 1979.

The impact of growth on the distribution of income can be analyzed at various levels, e.g., at the regional level, the inter-commune level or at various intra-commune levels. Our model is of the last type. Indeed, we will be concerned primarily with inequalities among the brigades of a commune and the analysis will be conducted both at the level of the team and the brigade. Team-level income of a brigade consists largely of income obtained from agricultural activities. In addition, however, there will be some income from side-line occupations, e.g., construction and transportation, animal husbandry and poultry farming. The brigade-level income of a brigade, on the other hand, arises from enterprises run by the brigade organization and these are predominantly industrial in nature. We will not be concerned with the impact of growth on inequalities among households of a team, although it is clear that differences among teams will have direct implications for income differentials between households belonging to the different teams.

55

It has been common in the literature on China to attribute changes over time in the distribution of income to the impact of socialist policies alone. While these policies undoubtedly have been of great importance, several structural factors also have been highly significant in affecting trends in inequality. The interaction of these structural factors determines the natural tendency of the commune system. That is, structural factors determine the endogenous behaviour of the system at the local level, and it is this behaviour that we wish to explore.

There are of course a large number of externally imposed constraints, rules and targets which rural collective units confront. They are part of the Chinese institutional framework and evidently affect economic behaviour. Yet teams and brigades retain considerable freedom of action and power for independent decision making. This is one of the features of the Chinese countryside that we try to incorporate into our model. A second, structural, feature is the technological relationship that governs production within the collective units. Both these features influence the growth process at the microeconomic level, although both are moderated by the given policy and institutional framework.

In this part of the monograph, economic policies play only a passive role; they will be discussed in some detail in Part Three. Instead, for the time being, we concentrate on an analysis of the hitherto ignored endogenous processes operating inside the commune system. The impact of policy variables on economic growth and income distribution will be postponed until we have a clear understanding of how the system would tend to perform if left to itself.

Our original interest in this subject arose from some puzzling observations made in the course of field investigations in the communes of rural China. The data we gathered on the extent of income inequality in Qie Ma and Wu Gong communes in Hebei Province for different benchmark years between 1966 and 1978 showed there was a noticeable decline in inequality over the period. In both communes, the poorer brigades also experienced a larger absolute increase in income than the richer brigades. This was shown in Tables 3:3 — 3:6 in Chapter 3.

The puzzling thing about these pronounced tendencies toward greater equality is that there were no obvious policies that could account for them. It was of course official policy to give preferential treatment to poorer units in allocating loans and grants, but this policy did not appear to be powerful enough to explain the sharp reduction in inter-brigade income differentials that we observed. This led us to consider the possibility that endogenous characteristics of the growth process could account for the phenomenon. In a third commune, however, the situation was rather different. In this commune — Cheng Dong People's Commune in Shanghai Municipality — inequality among teams and brigades, far from narrowing, increased perceptively between 1975 and 1978. This is shown in Table 4:1. Of course, the period covered in this case is very short, but it is clear that whatever endogenous explanation we might put forward will have to be capable of explaining cases where growth is accompanied by widening inequality as well as cases of declining inequality.

Table 4:1 Spread of Net Income per Worker at Team and Brigade Levels: Cheng Dong Commune, 1975 & 1978

Serial Number	Name of Brigade	Net Income per worker in yuan					
		in 1975 at:			in 1978 at:		
		Team Level	Brigade Level	Both Levels	Team Level	Brigade Level	Both Levels
1	Chang Chang	329.1	592.4	370.2	646.6	641.4	645.3
2	Yang Jia	331.2	797.7	415.4	620.2	993.0	738.1
3	Zhou Jia	400.8	1,207.9	581.4	712.2	1,834.5	1,043.9
4	Cheng Dong	313.6	510.9	351.8	588.0	762.2	632.3
5	Kao Qiao	270.2	912.1	414.6	661.7	1,068.8	795.2
6	Li Xin	312.0	746.9	379.4	575.6	1,342.9	765.4
7	Chen Qiao	260.5	566.3	308.6	563.0	718.7	598.1
8	Xu Wang	283.2	945.5	420.6	522.1	1,257.7	734.0
9	Wang Lou	292.6	524.8	338.4	493.2	1,245.2	643.4
10	Lin Cen	274.5	430.5	301.8	467.5	626.2	502.8
11	Zhang Gu	322.9	860.8	422.7	544.6	895.0	636.3
12	Xiao Hong	249.6	793.9	337.7	465.4	980.0	569.7
13	Wang Shi	291.1	496.3	355.8	522.1	745.1	593.1
14	Dong Chen	302.1	991.3	454.3	766.0	851.2	802.8
15	Zhan Ban	329.3	694.0	424.2	546.2	994.7	684.4
16	Chen Jia	294.6	545.0	339.8	636.9	744.6	670.4
	Mean Income (yuan)	303.6	726.0	387.3	583.2	981.3	691.0
	Income Range (yuan)	151.2	777.4	279.6	300.6	1,208.3	541.1
	Ratio of Highest to Lowest	1.61	2.81	1.93	1.65	2.93	2.08
	Coefficient of Variation	0.15	0.292	0.174	0.143	0.313	0.176

The processes through which income is generated and distributed within a brigade can be viewed as occurring in four distinct stages. First, labour and raw materials are combined, with the help of capital equipment, to produce physical output. This physical output, given the prices faced by the brigade, can be translated into a figure for the gross income of the brigade. If production cost, i.e., expenditure on raw materials used as current inputs, is deducted from gross income, one obtains the net income of the brigade. This corresponds to the value added in production. Second, disposable net income is obtained as a residual by deducting state taxes from net income.

Third, from this sum are withdrawn contributions to the public accumulation fund and the much smaller public welfare fund. After deducting collective accumulation from disposable net income, one is left with the amount that can be distributed among the members of the brigade in accordance with the distributional rules in force. Households will then decide how to divide their income between consumption and savings, but this decision does not enter into the model as we are interested in learning only how the collective economy behaves. Fourth, the amount dedicated to collective accumulation (including, for the sake of simplicity, the small sums allocated to public welfare) is then reinvested in enlarging the productive capacity of the brigade. This process involves investment in additional equipment as well as an increase in the brigade's requirements for working capital.

This four stage process is quantified in the four sections of Chapter 5 that follows. We first construct an aggregate productivity relationship that links production costs (or material inputs) to the resulting flow of net income. Then the tax function is discussed, followed by an analysis of the collective accumulation function. The relationship between fixed and working capital requirements is discussed in the final section of the chapter. In Chapter 6 we bring these four relationships together to form a simple growth model. We then use the model to investigate the impact of growth on the distribution of income at the local level. The predictive capacity of the model is subjected to a small test and we conclude Chapter 6 with a brief discussion of the fundamental role of economic policies in influencing the impact of growth on income inequality.

five

Components of the Model

The Aggregate Productivity Relationship

In this first section we will attempt to estimate an aggregate productivity function. This function describes the relationship between the brigade's production costs and its net income, and can thus be regarded as a statistical summary of the first stage of the growth process. In conventional terms, we are seeking a function which shows how value added and raw material costs are related. There are several methodological and statistical points which have to be taken into account when attempting to construct such a relationship and we will examine these points as they arise.

Consider Wu Gong Production Brigade, for which we obtained time-series data for both value added and production costs for the period 1958 – 78. These data are used to construct the relationship depicted in Figure 5:1. It can be seen in the figure that aggregate resource productivity, as measured by the ratio of net income (NY) to production costs (PC), declines over the period as production cost per capita (PC/N) increases. Such a relationship does not correspond to the text book case of diminishing returns to scale, for we are concerned here only with raw materials. Moreover, the function does not correspond exactly to the conventional proposition about diminishing returns to an input, since there is no presumption in our relationship that the levels of application of the other inputs are held constant.

The explanation for the observed decline in the productivity of raw materials is in fact somewhat unconventional, namely, structural changes that accompany the process of economic development within the brigade as a collective unit. It is important to recognize that the data for both production costs and net income are aggregates. They refer to the totals for both team and brigade

59

level activities. As the brigade develops, it also industrializes and these new industrial activities are carried out at the level of the brigade rather than within individual teams.

Industrial activities require far more investment in infrastructure than agriculture, and they also have a much higher raw material cost per unit of output. Hence a steady shift in the composition of a brigade's output in favour of industry has the effect of reducing the productivity of expenditure on raw materials. This does not imply, of course, that shifting into industrial activities is less rewarding than additional investment in agriculture, since it is the marginal rather than our average returns that are relevant. Furthermore, agricultural and industrial activities are not entirely independent sectors but are partly complementary. That is, the returns in agriculture are themselves partly due to the support provided by the brigade's industrial sector. All that we are arguing is that the development process, insofar as it leads to an increase in the use of raw materials per unit of output, has an inherent tendency to lead to a decline in the aggregate productivity of resources.

This effect of a structural shift in the composition of output can of course be accentuated by the operation of diminishing returns as conventionally understood. That is, additional doses of an input within individual activities at either the team or brigade levels might be associated with a decline in marginal productivity. For example, increased applications of fertilizer in some agricultural areas might exhibit diminishing returns. Should such an effect be present, there would be a second independent tendency for the productivity of raw materials to decline. Our time-series data do not permit us to test for this second effect, although some of our cross-section results shed some light on this.

Time-series data of the type obtained for Wu Gong Brigade were impossible to obtain for the other brigades of Wu Gong People's Commune. However, we were able to obtain data for all ten brigades of the commune for the years 1966, 1972 and 1978 and this enabled us to conduct an analysis using cross-section evidence.

In Figure 5:2 we plot the aggregate productivity relationship using pooled time-series and cross-section data. As can readily be seen, the nature of the relationship remains unaltered: productivity declines with increased expenditure on raw materials. Close inspection of the scatter diagram reveals that there are three over-lapping and successively flatter downward sloping curves for 1966, 1972 and 1978, respectively. This gives us some justification for using cross-sectional relationships as reflections of secular processes. That is, we assume implicitly that the different brigades of the commune confront a similar external environment and face roughly the same set of technologies and economic choices. What differentiates them from one another is the fact that they are at different points in the development cycle of a brigade. Given that we are dealing with collective units rather than with individual households, and that we are concerned not with a market economy but with a socialist institutional framework, such assumptions are not too unrealistic.

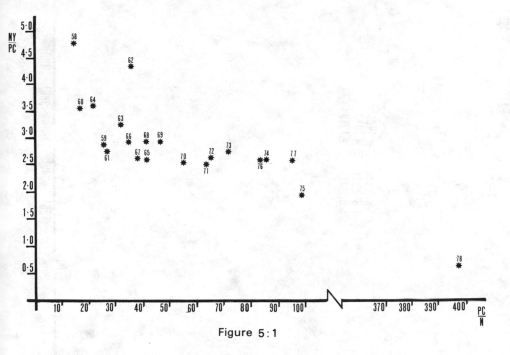

Figure 5:1

The relations plotted in Figures 5:1 and 5:2 are not purely technical or physical production relationships; they are essentially economic value relations. Both value added and raw material costs are influenced by the movement of input and output prices over time. However, over the period to which the data refer, prices were quite stable and hence a diagram based on current price values also represents a reasonable approximation of a relationship based on constant prices. The problem disappears entirely, of course, when pure cross-section data are used, as we will do later for Cheng Dong Commune.

The reader should note that the data for Wu Gong are always expressed in per capita terms whereas those for Cheng Dong are expressed in per worker terms. The reason for this is that in the case of Wu Gong data on employment are not available for the early benchmark years. Since labour force participation rates do not fluctuate markedly from one collective unit to another, it makes little difference to the nature of the results whether variables are measured in per worker or per capita terms.

Although we have cross-section data for all the relevant variables for the ten brigades of Wu Gong People's Commune for three benchmark years, our statistics are an aggregate of both team-level and brigade-level activities of each brigade within the commune. It is therefore not possible to compare the esti-mated functions for each level separately. This is a pity as a comparison of the team and the brigade level productivity functions might have cast some light on

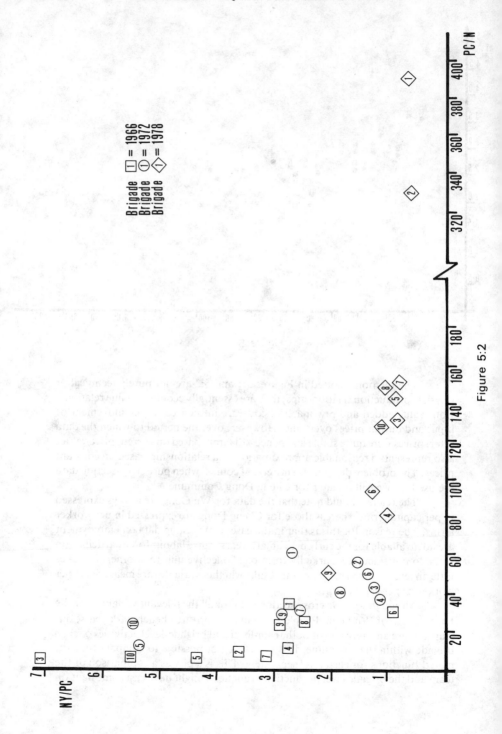

Figure 5:2

the operation of diminishing returns within different activities, e.g., agriculture and industry. In addition, a disaggregated savings function might reveal an interesting difference between the two levels.

In order to explore these issues more fully, we have selected Cheng Dong People's Commune as the focus of our enquiry. For this commune, we have data on all the variables which enter into the model, for 1975 as well as 1978. Data are available for both years for each of the sixteen production brigades of the commune separately at the level of the production team, of the brigade, and, putting the two together, at the joint level. This will enable us to see if the relationships that are estimated are reasonably stable when the data set is varied. The basic relationships also are estimated for the joint team-and-brigade level for the brigades of Wu Gung Commune. However, these results are tabulated but not discussed until a later section in which we compare the performance of the model in Cheng Dong and Wu Gong.

We can explore the aggregate productivity relationship in detail for Cheng Dong Commune with the help of Tables 5:1 to 5:9 at the end of the chapter. Tables 5:1 and 5:2 provide information on the structure of income by its components for each of the three levels of the commune. Thus, the team level accounts for only 23.26 per cent of the gross income as compared to 46.68 per cent of gross income originating at the commune level. The team level share of the net income is higher, being 32.5 per cent as compared to the commune level figure of 35.79 per cent. However, the team level share of gross expenditure, i.e., production costs, is only 14.68 per cent, and of accumulation, only 17.28 per cent, as against corresponding figures for the commune level which are four and three times higher, respectively. Thus, with the exception of its share of distribution, the commune level was generating a far greater proportion of the income, and absorbing an even greater proportion of the expenditure, than the team level in 1978. This testifies to the extremely high level of development already attained by Cheng Dong. The predominance of the commune level has arisen through a process which is easily recognized from the figures in Table 5:2. Thus, of the commune level net income, only a quarter is distributed while nearly one half is accumulated; at the team level, over three-fourths is distributed and less than one-fifth is accumulated. The figures for the brigade level fall between these extremes in all comparisons.

Table 5:3 indicates that the economic characteristics of the production activities at each of the three levels are very different. As we move from the team to the commune level, the value of fixed assets per worker, production costs per worker and net income per worker all rise very sharply, in fact by a factor of 6.35, 11.46 and 3.27, respectively. This reflects the fact that economic activity at the commune level is more capital and raw material intensive per worker as well as per unit of output.

Evidence on the relative importance of the different branches of economic activity by level is provided in Table 5:4 for the distribution of production costs and in Table 5:5 for the distribution of net income. The importance of agriculture declines, and that of industry rises as we move from the team level to the commune level. At one extreme, the commune level does not engage in any agricultural activities; at the other extreme, the teams have no industrial activities. The brigade, as usual, occupies an intermediate position, although industrial activities are far more important for the brigades than are agricultural ones. This evidence confirms the pattern that was observed at Wu Gong, namely, that there is a systematic process of structural change that occurs within the commune in the course of economic development.

Strong support for the argument that this structural change involves a reduction in the productivity of resources is provided by the data presented in Table 5:6. This table contains information on the ratio of net income to production costs in each major branch of activity at each of the three levels of the commune. Looking at the ratio for each level as a whole, it drops from 2.05 for the team to 0.9 for the brigade and then to 0.59 for the commune level. This decline is due to two factors. First, the higher levels have a greater share in those branches which have lower ratios. Thus, the productivity ratio is highest on average for sidelines, being 2.54. The ratio drops to 2.28 for agriculture as a whole and to 0.71 for all industrial activities. As we have already seen, the composition of output shifts from agriculture to industry as we move from the team to the commune level. However, there is a second interesting contributory factor. Every branch of activity displays a higher ratio at lower levels than at higher ones. Thus, for sideline activities, the productivity ratio drops from 3.22 at the team level to 1.92 at the brigade level and then to 0.86 at the commune level. A similar pattern is visible in the agricultural and industrial sectors. This could be interpreted to mean that, say, industrial enterprises at the brigade level differ systematically from those at the commune level as regards their pattern of resource use. It is noteworthy, too, that virtually every productivity ratio at the team level is higher than every ratio at the brigade level; similarly, the ratios are almost always higher at the brigade than at the commune level.

If one accepts that the process of development entails relative expansion of the industrial sector, and a gradual shift from team to brigade and commune level activities, then our cross-section productivity ratios certainly support our argument that resource productivity tends to decline over time for the commune as a whole. We can check the validity of this argument using time series data for 1971 – 78 for Cheng Dong. Tables 5:7 to 5:9 provide information on the growth of production costs, net income and the ratio of the two for each level of Cheng Dong Commune for the period mentioned. At first sight, Table 5:9 appears to contradict our argument, but closer scrutiny reveals that the numbers are consistent with the declining productivity hypothesis. It can be seen from Table 5:7 that after a sharp rise in 1973, the relative share of commune level activities declines steadily. The team and the brigade levels experience a sharp relative fall in 1973, after which the share of the team continues to decline, while that of the brigade rises consistently. Correspondingly, in Table 5:9, the overall productivity ratio falls dramatically in 1973, reflecting the sharp rise in the share of commune level activities. Subsequently, however, the overall ratio shows no clear trend. This can be explained by the fact that the rising importance of brigade level activities is achieved at the expense of both the team and the commune levels. The downward bias that a decline in the share of the team level would have imparted to the overall productivity ratio is cancelled by the upward bias generated by the simultaneous decline in the share of the commune level.

However, the data do not provide strong support for the notion that the productivity of resources declines within each level over time, or with the process of development. At the team level, the ratio displays no clear trend. The high figure of 3.05 for 1978 seems to impart an upward drift to the series, but this particular figure reflects in part the early effects of the new pricing policies in the countryside. The brigade level series shows little trend despite the steady increase in the level of per capita production costs. For the commune level, there does appear to be a sharp drop in the productivity ratio in 1973, when the per capita production costs at the commune level increased three-fold over their 1972 level, but the fall seems to have been only temporary and by 1975 the ratio had regained its original level. Of course, this evidence still is inconclusive, since the observed relative stability of the productivity ratio for each level over the period could be the product of an aggregation bias. That is, within each separate level there are different branches of activity and it is possible that declining productivity ratios could still apply to each separate activity over time.

Let us now turn to the results of our empirical exercises. These are presented in ten key tables, Tables 5:10 to 5:19 collected together at the end of the chapter, and it is important that these tables be understood correctly. Each table contains the estimates relating to a separate variation of the model's basic equations. For the moment we will restrict ourselves to equation 1 in each of the tables, as this equation relates to the aggregate productivity relationship. (The other equations will be discussed later in their appropriate sections.) The model has been estimated separately for the team level, the brigade level and then for the joint aggregated levels. Moreover, the model has been estimated with data for 1975, for 1978 and then for a pooled set of data for 1975 plus 1978. This procedure yields nine permutations. A tenth variation is estimated in Table 5:19 by using averaged values for the joint levels for both years. In some tables, different specifications of the same equation have been estimated. In such cases, the equations used for defining the model numerically have been identified by an asterisk.

Consider equations 1* in Tables 5:10 and 5:13 for the team level in 1975 and 1978 respectively: log NY = a + b log PC. The equations use a double log specification, as this was found to provide the best fit. The estimated coefficient is significant at the five per cent level, although the R^2 values are not high. The values of the coefficients are well below unity, implying that increases in production costs are accompanied by less than proportional increases in net income. Table 5:16 is based on the pooled data, and equation 1 seems to contradict this finding: the fit is very much stronger and the estimated coefficient is in excess of unity. However, this would appear to be the result of an aggregation bias introduced by the pooling of the two years, as equation 1* in Table 5:16 indicates.

The early effects of the price increases for agricultural products are felt in 1978. In order to separate these, we have used a dummy variable. This reduces the coefficient for production costs to 0.4, which is significant at the one per cent level. Corresponding results for the brigade level are provided in Tables 5:11, 5:14 and 5:17. They are similar in character to the results of the analysis at the team level. The dummy variable is not used for brigade level estimation since there are few agricultural activities at this level and hence price effects were of little importance. Results for the combined brigade and team levels are presented in Tables 5:12, 5:15 and 5:18 and it is clear that the fits are better than those obtained when examining the individual levels separately.

It appears from these results that there are diminishing returns to production costs at the team as well as at the brigade levels. This contrasts with our earlier finding (see Table 5:9) that the ratio of net income to production costs remained steady despite increased applications of inputs. The two results are not necessarily contradictory, however. The latter was based on aggregated data for Cheng Dong Commune as a whole, while the former results were obtained after looking at a scatter of different production teams. The two findings could be reconciled if the relative share of the teams with low initial levels of production cost increased over time. At the joint level, the results also incorporate the structural effect discussed at length earlier.

The average relationship indicated by the results is depicted in Figure 5:3.

The Tax Function

Let us now consider the second stage of the growth process. Having

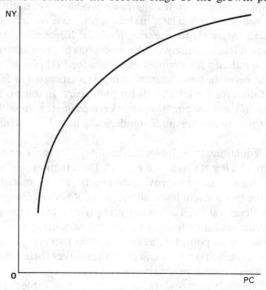

Figure 5:3

established an empirical relationship between the level of production costs and net income, we will now try to estimate a statistical relationship between the net income of a unit and its disposable net income. This involves estimating a tax function for each period and group of collective units that was previously considered.

The form of the tax function should be related to the nature of the tax sys_m actually encountered in the Chinese countryside. There is, however, no single tax rule but rather several variations around a common theme. Most commonly, teams pay an agricultural tax which is fixed in absolute terms. Hence with growth over time, the percentage of income paid as tax declines steadily. Such a tax rule, which is widespread in rural China, is regressive in its incidence. It is represented in Figure 5:4 by OAB, where OA represents the fixed tax liability. This fixed tax, however, accounts for a very small proportion of team income and consequently the regressive characteristic of the tax system is not a major problem or a cause for concern.

Recently, the government has decided to waive the agricultural tax liability of the poorest teams in China. One can conceptualize this by saying that the agricultural tax does not apply until team incomes reach a certain minimum level, depicted in the figure as OP. Once this income level is attained, however, the team must pay tax according to the earlier rule. This case is represented by OCDB, where OA = CD is the tax. Such a system implies the existence of a poverty trap, since a team with an income in the range PQ would have a lower disposable income than other teams with a smaller net income. That is, a team's disposable income would actually fall in absolute terms when its net income reached point P and it would not regain its best previous level of disposable income until its net income rose to point Q.

The industrial income of the commune is taxed on a different basis. Beyond a certain exemption level, indicated by OH, industrial enterprises pay taxes at a proportional rate. In fact, there are several kinds of taxes, but for the sake of simplicity we have depicted two cases only. In one, represented by OEF, a fixed proportional tax applies after the exemption level is reached. In the other, represented by OEG, a progressive tax is levied once income from industrial activities exceeds OH.

For the purposes of our model, however, we have used a simple proportional tax rule and assumed no income is exempt: DNY = aNY, where DNY is disposable net income per worker. This procedure greatly simplifies the complexities of the tax systems found in the communes we studied without entailing a significant loss of realism. This is especially true because taxes form such a small proportion of net income. The estimated tax function is described in equation 2* in each of the Tables 5:10 to 5:19, and the fit, not surprisingly, is very good.

The Collective Accumulation Relationship

The third stage in our analysis of the growth process consists of an

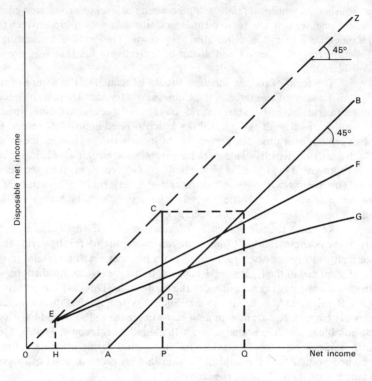

Figure 5:4

examination of collective accumulation. We will seek to establish an empirical relationship between disposable net income per worker and that part of it that is retained for collective accumulation. In our analysis, all disposable income that is not distributed is assumed to form part of collective accumulation. In fact, this is merely a simplifying assumption which is not strictly accurate. Some funds are retained for collective welfare activities and some others are used to finance such things as grain stocks held for contingencies. By far the largest proportion of retentions, however, is for the purpose of collective accumulation.

In making decisions about their savings rate, collective units operate within the institutional framework of the commune, and hence their choices inevitably are constrained somewhat by priorities set at a higher level. That is, teams and brigades are required to fulfil certain obligations, notably to ensure certain minimum consumption levels and to finance certain basic investments. However, this still leaves a fairly wide margin for choice, although the choices might be influenced by a general encouragement from higher levels either to accumulate more or to distribute more income. If common external influences were exerted on all collective units, one would expect them to move in the same general direction. In any one year, however, one would expect to find differences in the rate of accumulation from one team, say, to another. The issue is whether there is a systematic relationship between the disposable income of a team or brigade and its pace of accumulation. Our hypothesis is that there is.

As in the case of the aggregate productivity relationship, we can use the time-series data from Wu Gong Production Brigade to investigate the nature of this relationship over time. In Figure 5:5, the horizontal axis measures per capita disposable net income in yuan (DNY/N), while the vertical axis measures the proportion that is distributed $(1 - \frac{CA}{DNY})$. The observations for each of the years from 1958 to 1978 are indicated in the scattergram. The scatter reveals a very clear relationship: as per capita disposable income increases, the proportion of income distributed falls and consequently the collective accumulation ratio rises. It is interesting to note how accumulation behaved during the difficult period of 1958 – 61. There are exceptionally high saving and accumulation ratios in 1958 and 1959, followed by much lower ones in 1960 and 1961. Yet in all four years there was a roughly similar level of income. The last two years, indeed, display a savings behaviour that is consistent with the entire period that follows.

Figure 5:6 is a second scattergram. It is based on data from each of the ten brigades of Wu Gong People's Commune for each of the three benchmark years of 1966, 1972 and 1978. The pooled data in this scattergram reveal a similar pattern to that found in the previous figure. In applying our model to Cheng Dong Commune, however, we relied on our cross-section data of the brigades. We began by fitting a double log equation to the data, relating collective accumulation per worker (CA) to disposable net income per worker (DNy). The results are reported in equation 3 of Tables 5:10 – 5:16 and 5:19 and in equation 3.1 in Tables 5:17 and 5:18. A graphical representation of the estimating equation log CA = log a + b log DNy is shown in Figure 5:7. In every case the data fit the equation well and the coefficients are highly significant.

None the less, we decided not to use this equation but instead to substitute a second equation in which the collective accumulation ratio (CA/DNY) is related to the reciprocal of disposable net income: 1/DNY. The reason for rejecting the first version is that beyond a certain level of income, the estimated equation implies that collective accumulation will exceed disposable net income. This clearly is nonsensical. Our second version of the equation avoids this difficulty, although the statistical properties of the fitted equation are not quite as impressive. The nature of the function is depicted in Figure 5:8, where the savings ratio is shown to rise asymptotically towards a ceiling.

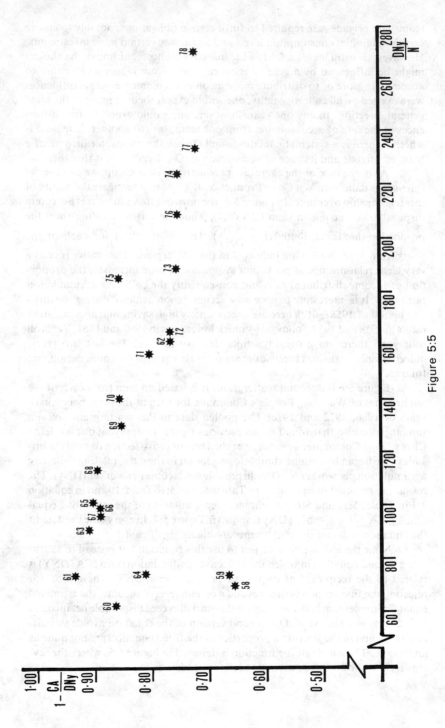

Figure 5:5

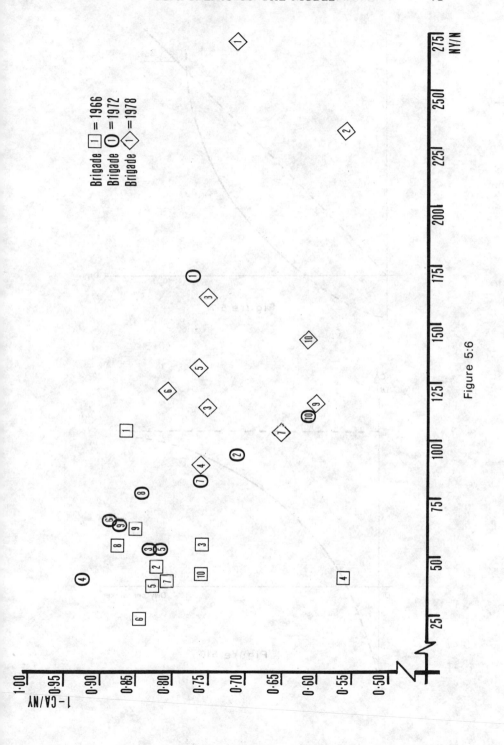

Figure 5:6

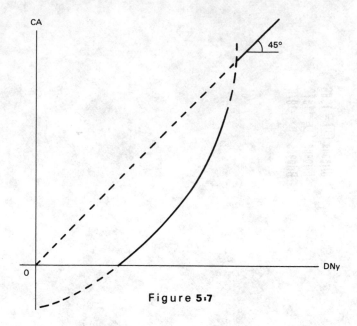

Figure 5:7

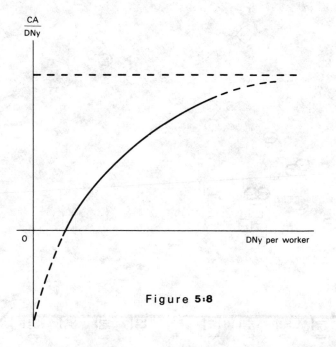

Figure 5:8

It will be noticed in Tables 5:17 and 5:18 that once again we have used a dummy variable in the equation based on pooled data for 1975 and 1978 at the brigade and joint levels. This was done to overcome an aggregation problem that arose from the fact that in 1978 savings ratios were consistently lower than in 1975. The reason for this, in turn, was the new policy of the government to encourage collective units to distribute a higher proportion of disposable income to the people in order quickly to raise their consumption. Our results suggest that the fall in the savings ratio was substantial, namely, about 16 percentage points. The aggregation problem does not arise in Table 5:19, of course, because here the results for 1975 and 1978 are not pooled but averaged together to form a single observation.

The conclusion of our investigation is that savings behaviour in Chinese communes typically is Keynesian. That is, higher levels of income per head normally are associated with a higher rate of saving and collective accumulation. This in itself would tend to increase inequality in the distribution of income, although it could of course be offset by other factors.

Fixed Capital and Production Costs

So far we have analyzed the relationship between production costs (or working capital) and the flow of net income; between net income and disposable net income, taking into account the incidence of taxation; and in the last section, between disposable net income and the annual rate of accumulation. It will be noticed that in each of these stages of the growth process, no role has been played by fixed capital. In this section we will introduce the missing element of fixed capital into our analysis.

So far it has been assumed only implicitly that production costs combine with fixed capital to generate the net income of the collective unit. Evidently, not all of the money that is accumulated collectively is used to augment the production cost or working capital fund. Some of it is spent on fixed capital. Hence the sum set aside for collective accumulation must be divided into two parts before the next round of an augmented growth process can start, one part being allocated to working capital and the remainder to fixed capital. The problem, then, is to discover the relationship between fixed and working capital.

An examination of the data from the 16 brigades of Cheng Dong Commune, by level and by year, indicated there was no systematic relationship between these variables. The ratio of one to the other fluctuated across teams and brigades as well as from one year to another. This, however, is not very surprising, since the ratio of fixed to working capital is greatly influenced by fluctuations in capacity utilization as well as by the discontinuous nature of investments in new enterprises at the team or brigade level. In Table 5:20 we present the values of the ratio of production costs to collective accumulation for three different levels and two different years. Since the variation is not very wide, we decided to use the average for both years and all levels of 0.44 in all of our arithmetical exercises. Had we chosen a different value for the ratio, the important qualitative results of the model would not have been affected. That is, the general findings of the analysis are not sensitive to the value of this particular ratio. The ratios in Table 5:20 are slightly different from those reported in Table 5:3 because of different averaging procedures used in computing the two tables.

Our model implies that the required amount of fixed capital was available in the initial round of the growth process to combine with production cost outlays to generate the net income of the unit. At the end of the first round, the sum set aside for accumulation is divided according to this average ratio between additional fixed capital and additional production costs. It follows, then, that production costs and fixed capital are applied in a fixed relationship throughout the model. Our use of the term production costs to the apparent exclusion of fixed capital is therefore slightly misleading. When the term production costs is used it should be understood to imply that working and fixed capital are being combined in fixed proportions in the process of production and growth.

Table 5:1 Distribution of Income Components by Level, Cheng Dong Commune, 1978

Income Component	All Levels	Commune	Production Brigade-run Enterprises	Production Brigade as Basic Accounting Unit	Production Team
Gross Income	100	46.68	20.09	9.97	23.26
Gross Expenditure	100	56.78	20.34	8.20	14.68
Net Income	100	35.79	19.83	11.88	32.50
State Tax	100	57.11	21.50	9.28	12.11
Distribution	100	18.60	19.19	13.36	48.83
Accumulation	100	51.85	20.03	10.84	17.28

Table 5:2 The Composition of Gross and Net Income by Level, Cheng Dong Commune, 1978

Income Component	All Levels		Commune		Production Brigade-run Enterprises		Production Brigade as Basic Accounting Unit		Production Team	
Gross Income	100		100		100		100		100	
Gross Expenditure	51.87		63.10		52.51		42.64		32.76	
Net Income	48.13	100.00	36.90	100.00	47.49	100.00	57.36	100.00	67.24	100.00
Of which:										
State Tax	7.24	15.05	8.86	24.03	7.76	16.34	6.74	11.75	3.77	5.61
Distribution	24.39	50.67	9.72	26.32	23.29	49.03	32.67	56.96	51.19	76.16
Accumulation	16.50	34.28	18.32	49.65	16.44	34.63	17.95	31.29	12.25	18.23

Table 5:3 Some Economic Indicators by Level, Cheng Dong Commune, 1978

Measure	All Levels	Commune	Production Brigade-run Enterprises	Production Brigade as Basic Accounting Unit	Production Team
Fixed Assets	100.00	37.12	28.23	17.32	17.34
Labour Force	100.00	17.37	19.13	12.05	51.44
Net Income as % of Fixed Assets	82.49	79.56	57.93	56.58	54.62
Production Cost as % of Fixed Assets	88.91	36.0	64.06	42.07	75.32
Net Income per Worker (yuan)	865	1,783	896	853	546
Production Costs per Worker (yuan)	932	3,048	992	634	266
Fixed Assets per Worker (yuan)	1,049	2,240	1,547	1,507	353

Table 5:4 Distribution of Production Costs by Level and Sector, Cheng Dong Commune, 1978

Sector	All Level	Commune	Production Brigade-run Enterprises	Production Brigade as Basic Accounting Unit	Production Team
Fishing	100.00	100.00	0.00	0.00	0.00
	(0.35)	(0.63)	(0.00)	(0.00)	(0.00)
Sidelines	100.00	64.41	10.36	5.91	19.32
	(9.10)	(10.32)	(4.63)	(6.55)	(11.96)
Agriculture	100.00	0.00	5.24	14.56	84.90
	(12.57)	(0.00)	(0.32)	(22.34)	(72.67)
Industry	100.00	70.61	22.78	6.61	0.00
	(63.17)	(85.73)	(77.20)	(55.60)	(0.00)
All Sectors	100.00	56.78	20.34	8.20	14.68
	(100.00)	(100.00)	(100.00)	(100.00)	(100.00)

1. Figures in brackets are column percentages.
2. The sector classification is not exhaustive.

Table 5:5 Distribution of Net Income by Level and Sector, Cheng Dong Commune, 1978

Sector	All Level	Commune	Production Brigade-run Enterprises	Production Brigade as Basic Accounting Unit	Production Team
Fishing	100.00	100.00	0.00	0.00	0.00
	(0.75)	(2.11)	(0.00)	(0.00)	(0.00)
Sidelines	100.00	36.09	12.85	10.76	40.30
	(15.13)	(15.20)	(9.55)	(13.61)	(19.17)
Agriculture	100.00	0.00	0.25	15.80	83.95
	(30.91)	(0.00)	(0.37)	(40.83)	(81.57)
Industry	100	54.94	34.32	10.73	0.00
	(53.10)	(81.26)	(89.51)	(47.65)	(0.00)
All Sectors	100	35.79	19.83	11.88	32.50
	(100.00)	(100.00)	(100.00)	(100.00)	(100.00)

1. Figures in brackets are column percentages.
2. The sector classification is not exhaustive.

Table 5:6 The Ratio of Net Income to Production Cost by Level and Sector, Cheng Dong Commune, 1978

Sector	All Levels	Commune	Production Brigade-run Enterprises	Production Brigade as Basic Accounting Unit	Production Team
Fishing	1.98	—	—	—	1.98
Sidelines	2.54	0.86	1.92	2.81	3.22
Agriculture	2.28	—	1.08	2.47	2.26
Industry	0.71	0.55	1.08	1.16	—
Animal Husbandry	0.02	0.34	0.04	− 0.34	− 0.13
All sectors	1.93	0.59	0.90	1.35	2.05

Table 5:7 Index Numbers of the Growth of Production Costs by Level, Cheng Dong Commune, 1971 – 1978

Year	All Levels	Commune	Production Brigade-run Enterprises	Production Brigade as Basic Accounting Unit	Production Team
1971	—	—	85.70	—	90.23
	(100)	(n.a.)	(n.a.)	(n.a.)	(n.a.)
1972	100.00	100.00	100.00	—	100.00
	(100)	(43)	(21.7)	(n.a.)	(35.3)
1973	200.28	313.09	127.8	—	106.61
	(100)	(67.3)	(13.9)	(n.a.)	(18.8)
1974	198.43	290.50	160.08	—	109.84
	(100)	(63)	(17.5)	(n.a.)	(19.5)
1975	197.70	279.91	177.70	—	109.85
	(100)	(60.9)	(19.5)	(n.a.)	(19.6)
1976	200.16	266.31	214.09	—	111.02
	(100)	(57.2)	(23.2)	(n.a.)	(19.6)
1977	229.16	320.34	214.04	100	87.85
	(100)	(58.28)	(19.63)	(8.97)	(13.12)
1978	235.44	320.65	227.80	93.88	101.05
	(100)	(56.8)	(20.3)	(8.2)	(14.7)

Figures in brackets are row percentages

Table 5:8 Index Numbers of the Growth of Net Income by Level, Cheng Dong
Commune, 1971 – 1978

Year	All Levels	Commune	Production Brigade-run Enterprises	Production Brigade as Basic Accounting Unit	Production Team
1971	—	—	70.33	—	76.33
	(n.a.)	(n.a.)	(n.a.)	(n.a.)	(n.a.)
1972	100.00	100.00	100.00	—	100.00
	(100.00)	(20.62)	(19.96)	(n.a.)	(62.55)
1973	111.56	147.63	137.47	—	93.51
	(100.00)	(26.16)	(23.58)	(n.a.)	(50.26)
1974	130.72	276.03	139.52	—	89.10
	(100.00)	(38.70)	(20.42)	(n.a.)	(40.88)
1975	145.76	164.99	170.46	—	95.35
	(100.00)	(38.40)	(22.38)	·(n.a.)	(39.22)
1976	157.40	268.15	229.54	—	100.76
	(100.00)	(33.69)	(27.91)	(n.a.)	(38.40)
1977	165.60	303.96	204.90	100.00	81.37
	(100.00)	(36.62)	(23.65)	(10.29)	(29.44)
1978	196.34	355.53	203.41	136.82	106.40
	(100.00)	(35.79)	(19.83)	(11.88)	(32.50)

Figures in brackets are row percentages

Table 5:9 The Ratio of Net Income to Production Cost by Level,
Cheng Dong Commune, 1971 – 1978

Year	All Levels	Commune	Production Brigade	Production Team
1971	—	—	1.83	2.65
1972	2.10	1.53	2.01	2.85
1973	1.64	1.25	2.09	2.71
1974	1.76	1.46	1.88	2.58
1975	1.85	1.53	1.97	2.69
1976	1.90	1.53	2.09	2.77
1977	1.80	1.51	1.97	2.81
1978	1.93	1.58	1.90	3.05

Table 5:10 Cheng Dong Commune: Growth Relationships

Data Level: Team
Year: 1975

Equation No.	Dependent Variable	Explanatory Variables					R^2	F	N
		Constant	Log Pc	Ny	Log DNy	$\frac{1}{DNy}$			
1*	Log Ny	3.0789 (2.39)	0.5077 (2.04)				0.23	4.18	16
2*	DNy			0.9267 (722.73)			0.99	—	16
3	Log CA	−8.2734 (−4.33)			2.0848 (6.15)		0.73	37.87	16
3*	CA/DNy	0.2470 (6.31)				−36.08 (−3.34)	0.44	11.195	16

PC = Production Cost per worker
Ny = Net Income per worker
DNy = Disposable Net Income per worker
CA = Collective Accumulation per worker

Table 5:11 Cheng Dong Commune: Growth Relationships

Data Level: Brigade
Year: 1975

Equation No.	Dependent Variable	Explanatory Variables					R^2	F	N
		Constant	Log Pc	Ny	Log DNy	$\frac{1}{DNy}$			
1*	Log Ny	2.3576 (2.07)	0.6368 (3.68)				0.49	13.59	16
2*	DNy			0.9496 (356.75)			0.99	—	16
3	Log CA	−4.8466 (−8.52)			1.6398 (18.74)		0.96	351.52	16
3*	CA/DNy	0.8386 (18.44)				−208.17 (−7.45)	0.79	55.54	16

PC = Production Cost per worker
Ny = Net Income per worker
DNy = Disposable Net Income per worker
CA = Collective Accumulation per worker

Table 5:12 Cheng Dong Commune: Growth Relationships

Data Level: Brigade and Teams
Year: 1975

Equation No.	Dependent Variable	Constant	Explanatory Variables				R^2	F	N
			Log Pc	Ny	Log DNy	$\dfrac{1}{DNy}$			
1*	Log Ny	1.7967 (2.41)	0.7334 (5.57)				0.68	31.08	16
2*	DNy			0.9354 (835.12)			0.99	—	16
3	Log CA	−8.7724 (6.25)			2.2626 (9.48)		0.86	86.89	16
3*	CA/DNy	0.6371 (9.48)				−130.29 (−5.56)	0.68	30.98	16

PC = Production Cost per worker
Ny = Net Income per worker
DNy = Disposable Net Income per worker
CA = Collective Accumulation per worker

Table 5:13 Cheng Dong Commune: Growth Relationships

Data Level: Team
Year: 1978

Equation No.	Dependent Variable	Explanatory Variables					R^2	F	N
		Constant	Log Pc	Ny	Log DNy	$\frac{1}{DNy}$			
1*	Log Ny	4.3522 (3.93)	0.3588 (1.81)				0.19	3.27	16
2*	DNy			0.9449 (784.13)			0.99	—	16
3	Log CA	−3.0426 (−2.98)			1.2246 (7.57)		0.80	57.42	16
3*	CA/DNy	0.2419 (7.25)				−24.13 (−1.35)	0.11	1.82	16

PC = Production Cost per worker
Ny = Net Income per worker
DNy = Disposable Net Income per worker
CA = Collective Accumulation per worker

Table 5:14 Cheng Dong Commune: Growth Relationships

Data Level: Brigade
Year: 1978

Equation No.	Dependent Variable	Constant	Explanatory Variables Log PC	Ny	Log DNy	$\frac{1}{DNy}$	R^2	F	N
1*	Log Ny	3.8512 (4.09)	0.4330 (3.18)				0.42	10.16	16
2*	DNy			0.8164 (54.94)			0.91	—	16
3	Log CA	−8.5244 (−4.21)			2.1365 (7.05)		0.78	49.82	16
3*	CA/DNy	0.8315 (10.91)				−321.93 (−5.61)	0.69	31.52	16

PC = Production Cost per worker
Ny = Net Income per worker
DNy = Disposable Net Income per worker
CA = Collective Accumulation per worker

Table 5:15 Cheng Dong Commune: Growth Relationships

Data Level: Brigade and Team
Year: 1978

Equation No.	Dependent Variable	Constant	Log Pc	Ny	Log DNy	$\frac{1}{DNy}$	R^2	F	N
				Explanatory Variables					
1*	Log Ny	3.9872 (5.43)	0.4104 (3.46)				0.46	11.95	16
2*	DNy			0.8969 (115.052)			0.95		16
3	Log CA	−8.7523 (−6.33)			2.1612 (10.04)		0.87	100.96	16
3*	CA/DNy	0.6120 (9.63)				−202.07 (−5.28)	0.66	27.88	16

PC = Production Cost per worker
Ny = Net Income per worker
DNy = Disposable Net Income per worker
CA = Collective Accumulation per worker

Table 5:16 Cheng Dong Commune: Growth Relationships

Data Level: Team
Year: 1975 & 1978 pooled

Equation No.	Dependent Variable	Constant	Log Pc	Explanatory Variables				R^2	F	N
				Ny	Log DNy	$\frac{1}{DNy}$	Dummy Variable			
1	Log Ny	-0.4407 (-0.62)	1.202 (9.20)					0.73	84.70	32
1*	Log Ny	3.6371 (4.72)	0.399 (2.65)				0.4852 (6.56)	0.89	123.31	32
2*	DNy			0.9411 (592.54)				0.99		32
3	Log CA	-6.4906 (-15.96)			1.7701 (26.02)			0.95	677.39	32
3*	CA/DNy	0.2775 (28.63)				-44.144 (-13.13)		0.85	172.45	32

PC = Production Cost per worker
Ny = Net Income per worker
DNy = Disposable Net Income per worker
CA = Collective Accumulation per worker
Dummy Variable: 1975 = 0; 1978 = 1

Table 5:17 Cheng Dong Commune: Growth Relationships

Data Level: Brigade
Year: 1975 & 1978 pooled

Equation No.	Dependent Variable	Constant	Log Pc	Ny	Explanatory Variables Log DNy	$\frac{1}{DNy}$	Dummy Variable	R^2	F	N
1*	Log Ny	2.8525 (4.32)	0.5696 (5.83)					0.53	33.93	32
2*	DNy			0.8638 (61.01)				0.88		32
3.1	Log CA	-4.8462 (-3.93)			1.6123 (8.62)			0.71	74.16	32
3.2	CA/DNy	0.71 (10.69)				-172.273 (-3.85)		0.33	14.86	32
3*	CA/DNy	0.8950 (18.51)				-244.05 (-8.35)	-0.1643 (-7.11)	0.76	44.98	32

PC = Production Cost per worker
Ny = Net Income per worker
DNy = Disposable Net Income per worker
CA = Collective Accumulation per worker
Dummy Variable: 1975 = 0; 1978 = 1

Table 5:18 Cheng Dong Commune: Growth Relationships

Data Level: Team and Brigade
Year: 1975 & 1978 pooled

Equation No.	Dependent Variable	Constant	Explanatory Variables					R^2	F	N
			Log Pc	Ny	Log DNy	$\frac{1}{DNy}$	Dummy Variable			
1	Log Ny	1.2517 (5.67)	0.8418 (10.63)					0.79	113.16	32
1*	Log Ny	3.0527 (6.02)	0.5114 (5.72)				0.3098 (4.93)	0.88	112.80	32
2*	DNy			0.9065 (162.67)				0.98		32
3.1	Log CA	-3.6493 (-5.05)			1.3784 (11.75)			0.82	137.98	32
3.2	CA/DNy	0.3762 (10.87)				-45.66 (-3.09)		0.24	9.56	32
3*	CA/DNy	0.6838 (11.92)				-146.766 (-7.36)	-0.1626 (-5.89)	0.65	27.49	32

PC = Production Cost per worker
Ny = Net Income per worker
DNy = Disposable Net Income per worker
CA = Collective Accumulation per worker
Dummy Variable: 1975 = 0; 1978 = 1

Table 5:19 Cheng Dong Commune: Growth Relationships

Data Level: Brigade and Team
Year: 1975 & 1978 averaged

Equation No.	Dependent Variable	Constant	Log Pc	Ny	Explanatory Variables			R²	F	N
					Log DNy	$\frac{1}{DNy}$				
1*	Log Ny	2.8765 (3.98)	0.5679 (4.65)					0.61	21.66	16
2*	DNy			0.9125 (193.94)				0.98		16
3	Log CA	−8.8050 (−8.35)			2.2176 (12.9583)			0.92	167.91	16
3*	CA/DNy	0.6343 (12.25)				−167.09 (−7.00)		0.77	49.06	16

PC = Production Cost per worker
Ny = Net Income per worker
DNy = Disposable Net Income per worker
CA = Collective Accumulation per worker

Table 5:20 The Relationship between Production Costs (PC) and
Fixed Assets (FA), Cheng Dong Commune

Level	k 1975	k 1978	k Both Years
Production Team	.48	.37	.42
Production Brigade	.66	.39	.46
Both Levels	.55	.38	.44

Note: $k = PC/(PC + FA)$

six

The Growth Process

The Complete Model

It is now possible to bring together the four stages discussed so far and present an integrated growth process. This can be done quite easily with the assistance of the four quadrant diagram in Figure 6:1. The line AA in the northeast quadrant is the aggregate productivity relationship; the northwest quadrant contains the tax relationship, BB; in the southwest quadrant is CC, the collective accumulation relationship; and finally, in the southeast quadrant, DD reflects the ratio by which additional accumulation is divided into fixed and working capital.

The process begins at W1, where OW1 yuan of production costs per worker are incurred in the unit. This is transformed through A1 on AA into OX1 yuan of net income per worker, and then through B1 on BB into Y1 yuan of disposable net income per worker. Given the collective accumulation behaviour of the unit, this implies a sum for accumulation equal to OZ1 on OZ. From this sum, one part, equal to Z1D1, is allocated to increased production costs (or working capital), the rest being allocated to the complementary requirements of fixed capital. The additional production costs (Z1D1 = W1W2) are then added to the original level OW1, and the second production period begins through the same stages as before.

By following the production process through successive rounds, it is possible to trace the growth path for any of the variables endogenous to the model. In what follows, we will focus exclusively on net income per worker. This simple model has the virtue of encapsulating and combining the various technological, behavioural and institutional features that have been discussed in Chapter 5. Moreover, as will be seen later, the model can readily be used to

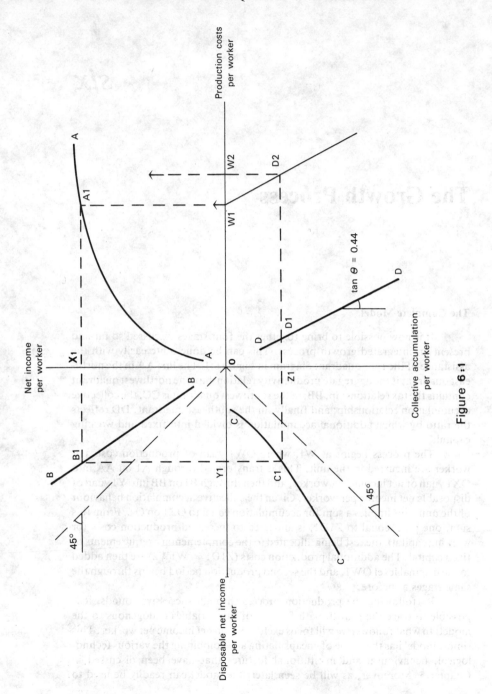

Figure 6:1

analyze the likely impact of a wide variety of policy changes emanating both from within and from outside the commune.

The Impact of Growth on Inequality: Some Simulations

Having constructed a simple quantifiable model that captures the essential economic features of a commune, we are finally in a position to examine one of the most important questions facing contemporary China, namely, the likely impact of growth on the degree of inequality at the local level. We shall try to shed light on this question by simulating the behaviour of a commune's economy using the model we have developed.

The model is highly flexible and lends itself easily to the type of simulation exercises we wish to undertake. There are several variants of the model depending on the choice of collective unit (team or brigade or the combined income of both) and base year (1975 or 1978 or pooled data or the average of the two years). The outcome depends to a certain extent, of course, on the choice of collective unit and base year and we shall comment later on some of the differences that result. The general conclusion, however, is robust and is not affected by the variant of the model that is chosen: there is a clear tendency for inequality to diminish in the long run, although in some cases it can increase significantly in the medium term.

To understand how this general conclusion is reached, let us begin by considering just one version of the model. This version consists of the three starred equations in Table 5:10 and the assumed constant proportion of working capital to fixed plus working capital of 44 per cent. This is all we need in order to be able to plot the path of net income per worker of the average production team in 1975. Now let us consider two teams, A and B, in both of which the same growth process described in Table 5:10 is assumed to apply. Let us also assume that in the base year net income per worker is twice as high in Team B as in Team A, viz., 400 yuan as compared to 200 yuan.

Given the starting income of each team we can trace their growth paths through as many production periods or years as we like. We can then see whether the ratio of their incomes has increased or declined during the period examined. That is, movements in this inequality ratio will indicate whether or not there is an endogenous tendency within the commune system for differences in income to diminish. The exercise can be repeated with different initial levels of income while holding the inequality ratio constant. Alternatively, one can alter the inequality ratio. In our simulations we used ratios of 2 : 1, 5 : 1 and 10 : 1. The full range of our results for Cheng Dong Commune is contained in ten sets of tables numbered Tables 6:1 to 6:10.

The results for our illustrative case are presented in Table 6:1. This case is based on team data from Cheng Dong Commune in 1975. Setting the initial inequality ratio at the low level of 2:1 and the level of income per worker at 400 and 200 yuan for Teams B and A, respectively, one can trace the evolution of the degree of inequality in the first column of the top section of the table. It can be

Table 6:1 A Model of Equalizing Growth: Results from Cheng Dong Commune: Production Teams: 1975

Alternative Base Year Levels of Net Income in Yuans per Worker for a Pair of Units

Inequality Ratio in Base Year set at 2:1

Production Periods	200–400	250–500	300–600	350–700	400–800	500–1000	750–1500	1000–2000	1500–3000
0	2.00	2.00	2.00	2.00	2.00	2.00	2.00	2.00	2.00
1	2.02	2.00	1.98	1.98	1.98	1.98	1.98	1.98	1.98
2	2.04	1.99	1.97	1.96	1.96	1.95	1.96	1.96	1.97
5	2.07	1.95	1.91	1.89	1.88	1.88	1.89	1.91	1.93
10	2.05	1.87	1.81	1.79	1.78	1.78	1.81	1.83	1.87
20	1.87	1.69	1.64	1.62	1.62	1.63	1.67	1.71	1.77
50	1.44	1.37	1.35	1.35	1.36	1.38	1.44	1.49	1.57

Inequality Ratio in Base Year set at 5:1

Production Periods	200–1000	250–1250	300–1500	350–1750	400–2000	500–2500	600–3000	700–3500
0	5.00	5.00	5.00	5.00	5.00	5.00	5.00	5.00
1	4.98	4.91	4.88	4.87	4.87	4.88	4.89	4.85
2	4.95	4.81	4.77	4.75	4.75	4.76	4.78	4.79
5	4.79	4.52	4.43	4.41	4.41	4.44	4.48	4.52
10	4.40	4.03	3.93	3.92	3.93	3.99	4.07	4.13
20	3.54	3.24	3.19	3.21	3.25	3.35	3.45	3.54
50	2.19	2.13	2.15	2.20	2.26	2.38	2.49	2.60

Production Periods	Inequality Ratio in Base Year set at 10:1			
	200 – 2000	250 – 2500	300 – 3000	350 – 3500
0	10.00	10.00	10.00	10.00
1	9.86	9.74	9.69	9.68
2	9.70	9.47	9.40	9.38
5	9.15	8.68	8.56	8.54
10	8.07	7.74	7.36	7.38
20	6.06	5.65	5.64	5.74
50	3.26	3.26	3.37	3.52

The results in this table have been generated using the estimated functions reported in Table 5:10.

Table 6:2 A Model of Equalizing Growth: Results from Cheng Dong Commune: Production Brigade, 1975

Alternative Base Year Levels of Net Income in Yuans per Worker for a Pair of Units

Inequality Ratio in Base Year set at 2:1

Production Periods	300–600	350–700	400–800	500–1000	600–1200	750–1500	800–1600	1000–2000	1250–2500	1500–3000	1750–3500
0	2.00	2.00	2.00	2.00	2.00	2.00	2.00	2.00	2.00	2.00	2.00
1	2.16	2.09	2.05	2.00	1.98	1.97	1.96	1.95	1.95	1.95	1.95
2	2.31	2.17	2.08	2.00	1.96	1.93	1.92	1.90	1.90	1.90	1.90
5	2.63	2.24	2.07	1.92	1.85	1.81	1.80	1.78	1.78	1.78	1.78
10	2.57	2.05	1.87	1.73	1.67	1.63	1.63	1.62	1.62	1.62	1.63
20	1.95	1.65	1.55	1.46	1.44	1.42	1.42	1.42	1.43	1.43	1.45
50	1.35	1.26	1.23	1.20	1.19	1.19	1.19	1.20	1.21	1.22	1.23

Inequality Ratio in Base Year set at 5:1

Production Periods	300–1500	350–1750	400–2000	500–2500	600–3000	700–3500
0	5.00	5.00	5.00	5.00	5.00	5.00
1	5.32	5.12	5.00	4.87	4.80	4.77
2	5.58	5.17	4.94	4.70	4.59	4.54
5	5.88	4.90	4.48	4.12	3.97	3.90
10	5.02	3.94	3.57	3.27	3.17	3.13
20	3.13	2.63	2.46	2.34	2.30	2.30
50	1.71	1.60	1.56	1.55	1.55	1.57

Inequality Ratio in Base Year set at 10:1

Production Periods	300–3000	350–3500
0	10.00	10.00
1	10.37	9.99
2	10.62	9.83
5	10.46	8.74
10	8.16	6.43
20	4.50	3.80
50	2.09	1.97

The results in this table have been generated using the estimated functions reported in Table 5:11.

Table 6:3 A Model of Equalizing Growth: Results from Cheng Dong Commune: Team & Brigade, 1975

Production Periods	Alternative Base Year Levels of Net Income in Yuans per Worker for a Pair of Units							
	Inequality Ratio in Base Year set at 2:1							
	250 – 500	300 – 600	350 – 700	400 – 800	500 – 1000	750 – 1500	1000 – 2000	1500 – 3000
0	2.00	2.00	2.00	2.00	2.00	2.00	2.00	2.00
1	2.17	2.11	2.07	2.05	2.01	1.98	1.97	1.96
2	2.36	2.21	2.13	2.08	2.02	1.97	1.94	1.93
5	2.86	2.40	2.20	2.09	1.98	1.88	1.85	1.83
10	3.19	2.37	2.09	1.97	1.84	1.74	1.70	1.69
20	2.59	1.95	1.76	1.67	1.59	1.52	1.51	1.50
50	1.60	1.40	1.34	1.31	1.28	1.26	1.26	1.27

Production Periods	Inequality Ratio in Base Year set at 5:1						
	250 – 1250	300 – 1500	350 – 1750	400 – 2000	500 2500	600 – 3000	700 – 3500
0	5.00	5.00	5.00	5.00	5.00	5.00	5.00
1	5.47	5.26	5.13	5.05	4.95	4.89	4.86
2	5.92	5.45	5.20	5.04	4.86	4.76	4.70
5	6.94	5.64	5.08	4.77	4.46	4.30	4.21
10	7.02	5.01	4.36	4.03	3.72	3.58	3.51
20	4.71	3.45	3.08	2.90	2.74	2.67	2.64
50	2.22	1.92	1.83	1.79	1.75	1.74	1.74

Production Periods	Inequality Ratio in Base Year set at 10:1		
	250 – 2500	300 – 3000	350 – 3500
0	10.00	10.00	10.00
1	10.76	10.33	10.07
2	11.54	10.52	10.02
5	12.75	10.32	9.29
10	11.90	8.48	7.37
20	7.09	5.20	4.65
50	2.81	2.45	2.33

The results in this table have been generated using the estimated functions reported in Table 5:12.

Table 6:4 A Model of Equalizing Growth: Results from Cheng Dong Commune: Teams, 1978

Alternative Base Year Levels of Net Income in Yuans per Worker for a Pair of Units

Inequality Ratio in Base Year set at 2:1

Production Periods	150–300	200–400	250–500	300–600	350–700	400–800	500–1000	750–1500	1000–2000	1500–3000
0	2.00	2.00	2.00	2.00	2.00	2.00	2.00	2.00	2.00	2.00
1	1.89	1.82	1.83	1.84	1.87	1.89	1.91	1.94	1.97	1.99
2	1.74	1.69	1.70	1.73	1.77	1.79	1.83	1.90	1.93	1.97
5	1.44	1.43	1.47	1.51	1.56	1.60	1.67	1.79	1.85	1.91
10	1.24	1.26	1.30	1.33	1.38	1.41	1.49	1.64	1.73	1.84
20	1.12	1.13	1.17	1.20	1.22	1.27	1.32	1.48	1.59	1.73
50	1.04	1.06	1.07	1.09	1.10	1.12	1.17	1.27	1.37	1.52

Inequality Ratio in Base Year set at 5:1

Production Periods	150–750	200–1000	250–1250	300–1500	350–1750	400–2000	500–2500	600–3000	700–3500
0	5.00	5.00	5.00	5.00	5.00	5.00	5.00	5.00	5.00
1	4.29	4.26	4.33	4.43	4.51	4.58	4.68	4.75	4.80
2	3.67	3.70	3.84	4.00	4.12	4.23	4.40	4.53	4.62
5	2.56	2.73	2.96	3.17	3.36	3.52	3.80	4.01	4.18
10	1.89	2.07	2.28	2.49	2.68	2.86	3.18	3.44	3.66
20	1.47	1.60	1.76	1.92	2.08	2.24	2.53	2.79	3.02
50	1.18	1.26	1.34	1.43	1.53	1.63	1.82	2.02	2.21

Production Periods	Inequality Ratio in Base Year set at 10:1						
	150 – 1500	200 – 2000	250 – 2500	300 – 3000	350 – 3500		
0	10.00	10.00	10.00	10.00	10.00		
1	8.36	8.37	8.58	8.79	8.96		
2	6.97	7.16	7.51	7.86	8.14		
5	4.57	5.06	5.60	6.07	6.50		
10	3.09	3.59	4.12	4.60	5.04		
20	2.16	2.55	2.95	3.34	3.71		
50	1.50	1.72	1.96	2.20	2.44		

The results in this table have been generated using the estimated functions reported in Table 5:13.

Table 6:5 A Model of Equalizing Growth:
Results from Cheng Dong Commune:
Production Brigades, 1978

	Alternative Base Year Levels of Net Income in Yuans per Worker for a Pair of Units			
	Inequality Ratio in Base Year set at 2:1			
Production Periods	500 – 1000	750 – 1500	1000 – 2000	1500 – 3000
0	2.00	2.00	2.00	2.00
1	2.08	1.98	1.96	1.96
2	2.16	1.94	1.91	1.92
5	2.32	1.84	1.80	1.82
10	2.33	1.68	1.65	1.69
20	1.89	1.46	1.45	1.51
50	1.33	1.21	1.23	1.28
	Inequality Ratio in Base Year set at 5:1			
Production Periods	500 – 2500	600 – 3000	700 – 3500	
0	5.00	5.00	5.00	
1	5.06	4.89	4.82	
2	5.09	4.76	4.64	
5	5.07	4.31	4.12	
10	4.55	3.57	3.40	
20	3.16	2.60	2.56	
50	1.77	1.68	1.70	

The results in this table have been generated using the estimated functions reported in Table 5:14.

seen that under our assumptions inequality increases slightly for about five years and then begins to diminish gradually. After 20 years the degree of inequality has declined noticeably and after 50 years it has fallen to a remarkable extent.

Assume, next, that the initial inequality ratio was 5:1 and that everything else was as before. The first column of the middle section of Table 6:1 indicates that inequality begins to decline immediately and at a rapid pace. Finally, were the initial degree of inequality greater still, as reflected, say, in a ratio of 10:1, the decline in the ratio would be even faster. This can be seen in the first column of the bottom section of Table 6:1.

The reader is now in a position to select the initial conditions that interest him and ascertain their implications by consulting the numerous tables that have been provided. Clearly it is not necessary for us to mention all our findings in the text. We can, however, attempt to summarize the overall results, and we will do this by focusing on the simulations based on pooled data.

Since it is of interest to see if the results of the analysis differ significantly when one shifts from the team to the level of the brigade, we will consider the

Table 6:6 A Model of Equalizing Growth:
Results from Cheng Dong Commune:
Teams & Brigades, 1978

Production Periods	Alternative Base Year Levels of Net Income in Yuans per Worker for a Pair of Units				
	Inequality Ratio in Base Year set at 2:1				
	400 – 800	500 – 1000	750 – 1500	1000 – 2000	1500 – 3000
0	2.00	2.00	2.00	2.00	2.00
1	2.07	1.99	1.96	1.96	1.97
2	2.12	1.97	1.90	1.90	1.92
5	2.19	1.87	1.78	1.80	1.84
10	2.06	1.69	1.61	1.65	1.72
20	1.66	1.43	1.42	1.47	1.56
50	1.24	1.18	1.20	1.24	1.33

Production Periods	Inequality Ratio in Base Year set at 5:1			
	400 – 2000	500 – 2500	600 – 3000	700 – 3500
0	5.00	5.00	5.00	5.00
1	5.00	4.82	4.78	4.77
2	4.98	4.63	4.56	4.56
5	4.72	4.08	3.99	3.99
10	3.94	3.30	3.28	3.33
20	2.70	2.43	2.49	2.57
50	1.64	1.62	1.70	1.77

The results in this table have been generated using the estimated functions reported in Table 5:15.

simulations based on the use of the starred equations in Tables 5:16 – 5:18. The corresponding simulations of the impact of economic growth on the distribution of income are presented in Tables 6:7, 6:8 and 6:9 respectively. In the top section of each of these tables the initial inequality ratio between a pair of units is assumed to be 2:1.

In the case of production teams, the results in Table 6:7 show that for an income range of 200 – 400 yuan, the degree of inequality rises marginally for three years and then begins to fall steadily. For any initial level of income higher than the ones selected, the inequality ratio begins to decline immediately and does so steadily. Turning to production brigades in Table 6:8, one can see that the broad pattern is similar but that movements of the inequality ratio are more accentuated. In three out of six cases, inequality increases at first, although for

Table 6:7 A Model of Equalizing Growth: Results from Cheng Dong Commune: Production Teams: 1975 & 1978

Alternative Base Year Levels of Net Income in Yuans per Worker for a Pair of Units

Inequality Ratio in Base Year set at 2:1

Production Periods	200 – 400	250 – 500	300 – 600	350 – 700	400 – 800	500 – 1000	750 – 1500	1000 – 2000	1500 – 3000
0	2.00	2.00	2.00	2.00	2.00	2.00	2.00	2.00	2.00
1	2.01	1.99	1.98	1.97	1.97	1.97	1.98	1.99	1.99
2	2.02	1.97	1.95	1.94	1.94	1.95	1.97	1.97	1.98
5	2.02	1.90	1.87	1.87	1.87	1.89	1.91	1.94	1.97
10	1.96	1.79	1.76	1.75	1.76	1.79	1.84	1.89	1.92
20	1.73	1.60	1.58	1.59	1.60	1.64	1.73	1.79	1.87
50	1.36	1.31	1.32	1.33	1.36	1.40	1.51	1.60	1.72

Inequality Ratio in Base Year set at 5:1

Production Periods	200 – 1000	250 – 1250	300 – 1500	350 – 1750	400 – 2000	500 – 2500	600 – 3000	700 – 3500
0	5.00	5.00	5.00	5.00	5.00	5.00	5.00	5.00
1	4.94	4.88	4.87	4.88	4.89	4.90	4.91	4.92
2	4.89	4.77	4.74	4.74	4.77	4.80	4.83	4.86
5	4.64	4.41	4.39	4.41	4.46	4.53	4.60	4.67
10	4.18	3.90	3.90	3.96	4.02	4.17	4.29	4.39
20	3.30	3.13	3.19	3.30	3.40	3.60	3.79	3.92
50	2.09	2.11	2.22	2.34	2.46	2.70	2.90	3.09

Production Periods	Inequality Ratio in Base Year set at 10:1				
	200 – 2000	250 – 2500	300 – 3000	350 – 3500	
0	10.00	10.00	10.00	10.00	
1	9.82	9.71	9.70	9.71	
2	9.63	9.43	9.40	9.43	
5	9.00	8.61	8.61	8.70	
10	7.87	7.43	7.50	7.68	
20	5.91	5.76	5.97	6.22	
50	3.34	3.55	3.83	4.13	

The results in this table have been generated using the estimated functions reported in Table 5:16.

Table 6:8 A Model of Equalizing Growth:
Results from Cheng Dong Commune:
Brigades 1975 & 1978

Production Periods	Alternative Base Year Levels of Net Income in Yuans per Worker for a Pair of Units					
	Inequality Ratio in Base Year set at 2:1					
	350 – 700	400 – 800	500 – 1000	750 – 1500	1000 – 2000	1500 – 3000
0	2.00	2.00	2.00	2.00	2.00	2.00
1	2.14	2.08	2.01	1.97	1.95	1.94
2	2.29	2.14	2.01	1.92	1.90	1.90
5	2.56	2.19	1.94	1.80	1.78	1.78
10	2.49	2.00	1.74	1.61	1.60	1.62
20	1.89	1.60	1.47	1.40	1.40	1.43
50	1.31	1.23	1.20	1.19	1.20	1.22

Production Periods	Inequality Ratio in Base Year set at 5:1				
	350 – 1750	400 – 2000	500 – 2500	600 – 3000	700 – 3500
0	5.00	5.00	5.00	5.00	5.00
1	5.51	5.06	4.88	4.79	4.76
2	5.41	5.04	4.71	4.58	4.51
5	5.56	4.70	4.13	3.94	3.88
10	4.70	3.74	3.27	3.13	3.10
20	2.96	2.51	2.31	2.28	2.29
50	1.66	1.56	1.52	1.53	1.56

Production Periods	Inequality Ratio in Base Year set at 10:1
	350 – 3500
0	10.00
1	10.20
2	10.30
5	9.90
10	7.70
20	4.30
50	2.04

The results in this table have been generated using the estimated functions reported in Table 5:17.

the income range of 500 – 1000 yuan the increase is negligible. Once the inequality ratio begins to fall, however, it falls more rapidly. In Table 6:9 team and brigade level incomes are combined and the reader can see that the results are qualitatively similar to those obtained for brigades.

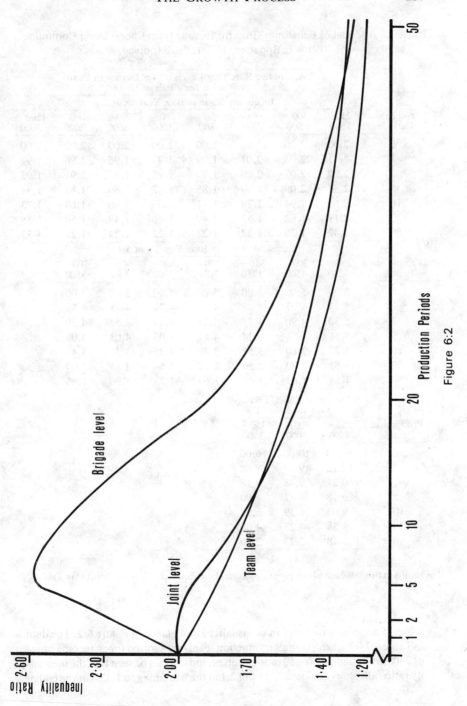

Figure 6:2

Table 6:9 A Model of Equalizing Growth: Results from Cheng Dong Commune: Teams & Brigades, 1975 & 1978 (pooled)

Production Periods	Alternative Base Year Levels of Net Income in Yuans per Worker for a Pair of Units							
	Inequality Ratio in Base Year set at 2:1							
	250 – 500	300 – 600	350 – 700	400 – 800	500 – 1000	750 – 1500	1000 – 2000	1500 – 3000
0	2.00	2.00	2.00	2.00	2.00	2.00	2.00	2.00
1	2.11	2.04	2.01	1.99	1.97	1.96	1.96	1.97
2	2.22	2.07	2.00	1.97	1.93	1.91	1.91	1.93
5	2.52	2.09	1.94	1.88	1.82	1.80	1.81	1.84
10	2.69	1.94	1.79	1.71	1.67	1.66	1.69	1.73
20	2.19	1.62	1.52	1.49	1.46	1.48	1.50	1.58
50	1.42	1.26	1.22	1.22	1.22	1.24	1.28	1.33

Production Periods	Inequality Ratio in Base Year set at 5:1						
	250 – 1250	300 – 1500	350 – 1750	400 – 2000	500 – 2500	600 – 3000	700 – 3500
0	5.00	5.00	5.00	5.00	5.00	5.00	5.00
1	5.17	4.97	4.88	4.82	4.79	4.78	4.79
2	5.30	4.90	4.73	4.64	4.59	4.58	4.59
5	5.56	4.56	4.24	4.11	4.03	4.03	4.07
10	5.27	3.80	3.50	3.40	3.35	3.39	3.43
20	3.61	2.70	2.56	2.52	2.54	2.61	2.69
50	1.89	1.69	1.68	1.69	1.73	1.80	1.86

Production Periods	Inequality Ratio in Base Year set at 10:1		
	250 – 2500	300 – 3000	350 – 3500
0	10.00	10.00	10.00
1	10.12	9.77	9.60
2	10.21	9.48	9.18
5	10.18	8.42	7.90
10	9.00	6.59	6.12
20	5.58	4.23	4.08
50	2.48	2.27	2.30

The results in this table have been generated using the estimated functions reported in Table 5:18.

The general pattern can be visualized at a glance in Figure 6:2. The data in Table 6:7 for Cheng Dong's production teams are plotted for an income range of 350 – 700 yuan and for 50 production periods. It can be seen that the inequality ratio falls slowly but steadily from 2:1 in the beginning to 1.33:1 at the end of

Table 6:10 A Model of Equalizing Growth: Results from Cheng Dong Commune: Teams & Brigades, 1975 & 1978 (averaged)

	Alternative Base Year Levels of Net Income in Yuans per Worker for a Pair of Units						
	Inequality Ratio in Base Year set at 2:1						
Production Periods	300 – 600	350 – 700	400 – 800	500 – 1000	750 – 1500	1000 – 2000	1500 – 3000
0	2.00	2.00	2.00	2.00	2.00	2.00	2.00
1	2.16	2.09	2.04	1.99	1.97	1.96	1.96
2	2.31	2.16	2.06	1.99	1.93	1.91	1.92
5	2.78	2.26	2.07	1.91	1.82	1.80	1.81
10	3.23	2.16	1.92	1.75	1.66	1.66	1.68
20	2.67	1.76	1.60	1.50	1.46	1.46	1.50
50	1.56	1.31	1.26	1.23	1.22	1.23	1.27

	Inequality Ratio in Base Year set at 5:1						
Production Periods	300 – 1500	350 – 1750	400 – 2000	500 – 2500	600 – 3000	700 – 3500	
0	5.00	5.00	5.00	5.00	5.00	5.00	
1	5.29	5.09	4.79	4.86	4.80	4.78	
2	5.56	5.12	4.90	4.70	4.60	4.57	
5	6.23	4.98	4.52	4.17	4.05	4.01	
10	6.43	4.23	3.73	3.41	3.32	3.30	
20	4.40	2.90	2.64	2.50	2.48	2.49	
50	2.03	1.72	1.67	1.64	1.67	1.70	

	Inequality Ratio in Base Year set at 10:1	
Production Periods	300 – 3000	350 – 3500
0	10.00	10.00
1	10.34	9.96
2	10.66	9.84
5	11.27	9.06
10	10.76	7.14
20	6.59	4.39
50	2.60	2.21

The results in this table have been generated using the estimated functions reported in Table 5:14.

50 periods. Brigade level incomes behave rather differently, however. The data in Table 6:8 indicate that for an income range of 350 – 700 yuan, the inequality index rises sharply for six periods (from 2:1 to 2.6:1) and then falls equally sharply for the next 14 periods. By the end of 50 production periods it has

declined to 1.31:1. Finally, combining brigade and team level incomes, the data in Table 6:9 indicate that for the same range of incomes, the inequality ratio remains essentially constant for two years, falls quite rapidly for the next 18 years and thereafter continues to decline gently, reaching a ratio of 1.22:1 after 50 production periods. That is, in 50 production periods inequality declines by nearly 40 per cent.

There are two major influences on the behaviour of the inequality ratio in our analysis. First, there is the equalizing influence of the aggregate productivity function. Secondly, there is the disequalizing impact of the collective accumulation relationship.

The equalizing effects of the aggregate productivity function are stronger in the earlier stages of the growth process than in the later, since at low levels of application the return to an incremental increase in material inputs will be high. The disequalizing effects of the accumulation function, however, also are more powerful in the earlier rather than later stages. The reason for this is that the function implies a sharply increasing savings ratio at low levels of income and relative stability of the ratio at high levels of income. Thus in the earlier years of the growth process the richer units accumulate faster and hence tend to grow richer faster whereas in the later years the rate of accumulation of the rich stabilizes while that of the poor increases, and hence differences in levels of income per worker and per head begin to decline. The movement over time of the inequality ratio consequently depends upon the relative importance of these two effects, and this can only be determined empirically in a model such as ours.

Viewed in this way, it is hardly surprising that the onset of the equalizing phase is earlier for the production team than for the brigades. There are fewer opportunities at the level of the team to escape diminishing returns to raw materials. Moreover, the disequalizing influence of accumulation also is much weaker at the team level. The reason for this is that only about a fifth of the net income of the team is saved, as compared to the much higher proportion saved at the level of the brigade. When brigade and team level incomes are combined the outcome depends largely on the relative importance of brigade level activities as against team level ones. In Cheng Dong the brigade is of increasing importance in generating income and consequently the behaviour of the inequality ratio for team and brigade level incomes combined tends to be more similar to that of the brigade than to that of the team.

In general terms, however, the most important finding of our analysis is that the extent of inequality between collective units within a commune can be expected to diminish in the long run, even if not always in the medium run. This reduction occurs not as a result of government policy but as a consequence of the structural characteristics of the commune itself. The equalizing tendency is inherent in the growth process and is not dependent upon active redistributive policies. Indeed, such policies have deliberately played no role in our model. However, it should be noted that while all the evidence indicates there is a secular tendency for inequality to decline with growth, the reduction in inequality may not be very significant for as long as 20 years. For example, starting with

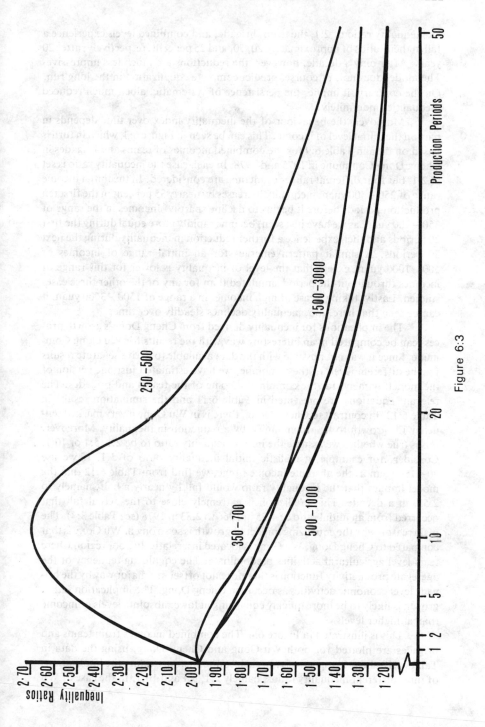

Figure 6:3

an inequality ratio of 2:1, the team, brigade, and combined levels experience a fall in their ratios of approximately 20, 50, and 25 per cent, respectively, after 20 years. After only a decade, however, the reductions are much less impressive. The model does not, of course, predict complete equalization in the long run. On the contrary, it implies the persistence of systematic, albeit much reduced inequalities indefinitely.

Moreover, the behaviour of the inequality index over time depends in part on the initial level of income. This can be seen in Figure 6:3, which in turn is based on data in Table 6:9 for the combined incomes of teams and brigades in Cheng Dong Commune in 1975 and 1978. In each case the inequality ratio is set at 2:1, but four different ranges of income are considered. In the initial income range of 250 – 500 yuan, inequality increases by nearly 35 per cent in the first ten production periods before it begins to decline sharply. Incomes in the range of 350 – 700 yuan, as we have just seen, become rapidly more equal during the first 20 periods and then experience a further reduction in inequality during the next 30 periods. A similar pattern emerges for an initial range of incomes of 500 – 1000 yuan, except that the level of inequality is lower for this range of incomes throughout the period simulated than for any of the other three cases studied. Lastly, taking a case of high incomes in a range of 1500 – 3000 yuan, it can be seen that here, too, inequality declines steadily over time.

The implications for inequality derived from Cheng Dong's growth process can be compared in an interesting way with the results for Wu Gong Commune. Since it was not possible with the data available to derive separate results for the different levels of the commune, we have estimated just one version of the model, namely, for the combined income of the teams and brigades. The relevant equations are presented in Table 6:11 and the simulation results in Table 6:12. In contrast to Cheng Dong, there is in Wu Gong a very marked tendency for growth to be accompanied by a reduction in inequality. Moreover, this is true whether we assume the initial inequality ratio to be 2:1, 5:1 or 10:1. Consider, for example, a realistic initial inequality ratio of 5:1. If we use 30 – 150 yuan as the absolute income range, we find from Table 6:12 that the model implies that the inequality ratio would fall by nearly a half, namely to 2.58, in a decade. This prediction is extremely close to the actual fall that occurred from an initial ratio of 4.25 in 1966 to 2.83 in 1978 (see Table 3:3). The main reason why the equalizing impact of growth is so strong in Wu Gong is that compared to Cheng Dong, Wu Gong is located in a relatively poor region where team level agricultural activities predominate. The equalizing tendency of the aggregate productivity function is therefore not offset in a major way by the brigade level economic activities as occurs in Cheng Dong. The implication is that growth is likely to be more quickly equalizing at lower absolute levels of income than at higher levels.

This is illustrated in Figure 6:4. The combined incomes from teams and brigades are plotted for both Wu Gong and Cheng Dong, using the data in Tables 6:12 and 6:9 respectively. In each commune, we explore the implications of three different inequality ratios, namely 2:1, 5:1 and 10:1. In the case of Wu

Table 6:11 Wu Gong Commune: Growth Relationships:
Teams & Brigades, 1966 & 1972 & 1978

Equation No.	Dependent Variable	Constant	Explanatory Variables				R^2	F	N
			Log Pc	Ny	Log DNy				
1	Log Ny	2.7088 (12.42)	0.4480 (7.93)				0.69	62.91	30
2	DNy	−3.9249 (−11.65)		0.9981 (325.04)			0.99	10.57×10^4	30
3	Log CA	−2.7262 (−5.67)			1.2927 (11.70)		0.83	136.93	30

PC = Production Cost per capita
Ny = Net Income per capita
DNy = Disposable Net Income per capita
CA = Collective Accumulation

Table 6:12 A Model of Equalizing Growth: Results from Wu Gong Commune:
Teams & Brigades, 1966 & 1972 & 1978

Production Periods	Alternative Base Year Levels of Net Income in Yuans per Worker for a Pair of Units							
	Inequality Ratio in Base Year set at 2:1							
	10 – 20	20 – 40	30 – 60	40 – 80	50 – 100	60 – 120	100 – 200	150 – 300
0	2.00	2.00	2.00	2.00	2.00	2.00	2.00	2.00
1	1.90	1.87	1.89	1.90	1.91	1.92	1.94	1.96
2	1.80	1.77	1.80	1.82	1.84	1.86	1.90	1.92
5	1.55	1.56	1.60	1.64	1.68	1.71	1.78	1.83
10	1.33	1.37	1.42	1.47	1.51	1.54	1.58	1.71
20	1.18	1.21	1.26	1.30	1.34	1.37	1.47	1.55
50	1.07	1.09	1.11	1.14	1.16	1.18	1.26	1.33
	Inequality Ratio in Base Year set at 5:1							
Production Periods	10 – 50	20 – 100	30 – 150	40 – 200	60 – 300			
0	5.00	5.00	5.00	5.00	5.00			
1	4.39	4.42	4.51	4.58	4.68			
2	3.87	3.96	4.12	4.24	4.41			
5	2.83	3.06	3.31	3.50	3.78			
10	2.06	2.33	2.58	2.79	3.11			
20	1.55	1.76	1.95	2.13	2.41			
50	1.21	1.32	1.42	1.52	1.70			
	Inequality Ratio in Base Year set at 10:1							
Production Periods	10 – 100	20 – 200	30 – 300					
0	10.00	10.00	10.00					
1	8.43	8.61	8.86					
2	7.16	7.54	7.94					
5	4.77	5.48	6.08					
10	3.13	3.84	4.44					
20	2.08	2.59	3.05					
50	1.42	1.67	1.90					

The results in this table have been generated using the estimated functions reported in Table 6.11.

Gong we assume the initial range of incomes is 10 – 20 yuan, 10 – 50 yuan and 10 – 100 yuan; in Cheng Dong the assumed range is 250 – 500, 250 – 1250 and 250 – 2500 yuan.

The behaviour of the inequality ratio is far from being identical in the two communes. In Cheng Dong inequality increases in every case, and when the inequality ratio is set at 2:1, the degree of inequality actually is higher after 20 periods than at the beginning. In Wu Gong, in contrast, inequality declines steadily regardless of the initial inequality ratio. Consider, for example, an i uality ratio of 2:1. In Wu Gong the ratio declines 5 per cent in the first iod, and by over 40 per cent in 20 periods. This is a remarkable performance r a commune of roughly average income such as Wu Gong.

A Small Test of the Validity of the Model

We have shown that changes in the degree of inequality in Wu Gong Commune in the period 1966 – 78 are similar to those one would expect on the basis of our model. This is comforting but it does not constitute a formal test of the validity of the model. All that we have shown so far is that the model fits the data from which it is derived reasonably accurately. In order to test the empirical validity of the model it is necessary to make a prediction for a range of observations which falls outside the set of data from which the model is itself estimated. Unfortunately, there are not enough data with which to conduct such a test on an extensive scale. It is possible, however, to conduct one small test.

Data are available for Cheng Dong Commune for all three levels — production team, brigade and the combined income of brigades and teams — for both 1975 and 1978. This was a period when there were few changes in government economic policies which could disturb Cheng Dong's underlying tendencies. Hence we can use the estimated equations based on the 1975 data (see Tables 5:10 – 5:12) to see how closely the predictions based upon them (as reported in Tables 6:1 – 6:3) conform to the observed changes in the inequality ratio between 1975 and 1978 (as reported in Table 4:1).

Using a base year absolute income comparison of 200 to 400 yuan, the model predicts that team level income per worker would rise from 2:1 to 2.05:1. In comparison, the actual inequality ratio in Cheng Dong in 1975, at the team level, was 1.61:1. Three years later, in 1978, it had increased slightly to 1.65:1. This is what the model would lead us to expect. The model also predicts that brigade level income, and the combined income of team and brigade level activities, also would become fractionally less equal. Again, actual experience conforms to this pattern.

We do not offer this as a conclusive test of the empirical validity of our model. Nevertheless, it is reassuring to find that the model passes the only test of its validity that we have been able to devise. Clearly more work needs to be done with additional information, but for the time being at least, our conclusions about the endogenous behaviour of the commune system appear to be valid.

The Role of Policies

One of the characteristics of the rural economy of contemporary China is a tendency for the productivity of resources to decline. We are able to account

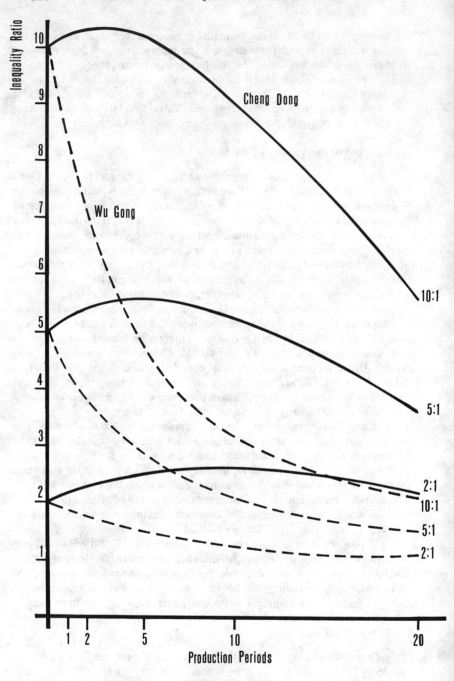

Figure 6:4

for this at the level of the commune with our aggregate productivity function. It would be interesting to know whether our structural explanation for the decline in productivity also applies at the county and regional levels. Unfortunately, lack of data prevents us from pursuing the issue further, but it would be surprising if our analysis had no validity in a wider context.

The process of equalizing growth that we have analyzed must not be confused with other, entirely separate, processes or policies which might enable poorer collective units to grow faster over time than richer ones. There is, in fact, one particular reason why poorer units might perform above average: the presence of unused or slack resources. That is, poor units (teams or brigades) are more likely than richer units to have unutilized local resources. Indeed, the latter may be richer in part because they have managed to find a productive use for their slack resources. But the mere fact that the richer units have used up their slack resources may mean that in future they are likely to grow less rapidly. Poorer units, in contrast, might be able in future to use their slack resources to achieve faster rates of growth. If so, inequality would diminish.

This effect is different from the one we have analyzed. We have argued that the productivity of expenditure on resources (or production costs) is higher at lower levels of income than at higher ones. The argument here, however, is that the quantity of resources available for growth is greater, or at least potentially is greater, at lower levels of income. The possibility arises that the productivity of resources on poor units may not be as high as it appears to be, since it may be that in fact slack resources are being used to increase income but are not valued as a production cost. That is, output may be correctly measured but the value of material inputs may be understated, and consequently the productivity of resources may be exaggerated. There is no way of knowing at present whether this is actually happening, but we must note that to the extent that it is, a process leading to a reduction in slack resources would be disguised as a decline in the productivity of resources.

This argument is plausible in the case of Wu Gong, but it is less likely to apply in a relatively rich commune such as Cheng Dong. The reason for this is that in rich communes slack resources are likely to have been used up already. Thus our evidence from Cheng Dong almost certainly indicates declining productivity of resources and not slack resources.

The structural tendencies we have identified as favouring income equalization over time are independent of the operation of specific policies designed to achieve greater equality. We do not argue, however, that such policies are unimportant. Indeed, policy interventions can be more significant than the structural tendencies that have preoccupied us. Nevertheless, our model sheds some light on a hitherto unexplored aspect of the commune system.

Moreover, policy changes can be introduced into the model in several ways, and the likely impact of changed policies on the distribution of income can be estimated, at least approximately through a process of simulation. For example, the recent changes in the structure of relative prices in rural areas could be handled very easily. All one would have to do is estimate a new aggregate productivity relationship using the new set of prices. In general terms, the new price policies are likely to push the curve AA in Figure 6:1 outwards, since the richer teams with a relatively high marketable surplus are likely to gain more than poorer teams. This implies, too, that the tendency for productivity to decline would be weakened and hence one of the major forces reducing inequality over time would become less powerful.

Other policies, such as changes in tax rules or the introduction of new guidelines for accumulation, can be integrated into the model quite readily. Of course, there are several other policies designed to promote growth with equality that cannot be incorporated so easily. This merely underlines our earlier point that the processes analyzed in our model operate in a given policy and institutional environment. The consequences of changing the environment is another subject entirely.

PART THREE

STRATEGIES FOR ECONOMIC DEVELOPMENT IN RURAL CHINA

seven

Rural Policies: The Broad Picture

In this and the next two chapters we are concerned with economic policies devised for rural development in China. The subject is vast and no treatment of it can aspire to being complete or comprehensive. Therefore we have little choice but to sacrifice depth of coverage for width and concentrate on the most important aspects of the topic. In the case of most countries, it might have been adequate to evaluate the operation of economic policies within the prevalent institutional framework. For socialist China, however, it is necessary to view the existing institutional framework as itself a product of policy. This is true of the present as well as of the past. That is, it is not justifiable today, as it might well have been until recently, to regard the post-1949 Chinese institutional structure as providing an unchanging framework within which economic policies operate: recent events have underlined the point that the institutional features of the countryside are themselves open to fundamental modification, mutation or outright substitution as part of new policy initiatives. We will begin, therefore, with a brief outline of the institutional framework that was prevalent in rural China prior to the recent extensive changes. Since, however, this framework is itself a consequence of policy and not merely an exogenous political constant (as is so often the case in the rural sector of non-socialist economies), it is necessary to provide a prior statement of the fundamental objectives of policy.

Implicit in the drive to construct a socialist society were the twin aims of achieving a substantial rate of growth and an equitable distribution of income. It was felt by the Chinese leadership that concentrating on the fastest road to economic growth cut too many socialist corners and thus seriously jeopardized safe arrival at the desired destination. Hence, with the exception of a brief interlude in the early 1960s, and in contrast to other socialist countries, the growth objective was never accorded primacy in the Chinese strategy of development.

In other words, until very recently, a feature of the Chinese strategy was a high rate of discount of future income, and this placed a strong limit on the level of acceptable short-run income sacrifices for projected long-run gains. Furthermore, all economic growth was required to reflect itself directly in an improvement in the standard of living of the Chinese peasantry. Given the predominant position of the rural sector in China, this implied that economic growth would have to be generated through a massive effort at a modernization of the countryside where the bulk of the Chinese people live and work. Thus, in terms of sectoral priorities, rural development came to enjoy pride of place.

If China's treatment of the growth objective was novel, especially in contrast with the early experience of the Soviet Union inside the socialist camp, and that of India outside it, its response to the distributional objective was no less remarkable. In a socialist society there is more to the objective of curbing economic inequality than lowering the ceiling for the rich and raising the guaranteed floor levels of income for the poor. It is also necessary that incomes should be earned and distributed in accordance with rules which do not violate socialist principles. Hence, it was necessary to root out income inequalities arising from the surviving vestiges of "bourgeois rights". This did not mean that the new distributional rules would produce identical incomes for all, but that incomes would have to be earned and related to the quantity and quality of work undertaken. However, in a country as geographically diverse as China, a peasant in the water-abundant south could earn a multiple of the income of a peasant in the dry hinterland. Moreover, in common with most Third World societies, the Chinese income structure was biased heavily in favour of urban workers, as well as those who worked with their brains rather than their muscles. Socialist policy for achieving the distributional objective therefore hinged upon an assault on the inequalities between peasant and peasant, between peasant and worker, and between the manual and the brain worker. Of course, a fundamental precondition for success on both the growth and distributional fronts was the construction of an appropriate new socialist institutional structure in the countryside to replace the one that was demolished in the course of the revolution.

The Institutional Framework

China is a socialist country, by far the largest in the world, and her agricultural sector is organized on the basis of socialist principles. There are no landless labourers working for wages. There are no sharecroppers dividing the harvest with the landowner. Indeed there are no private landlords or farms owned by large private corporations. All these features of capitalist agriculture are absent from the Chinese countryside. In their place has been established a system of collective agriculture in which cooperation for mutual advantage has replaced the principle of competition.

The present institutional framework did not spring up suddenly and fully formed the day after liberation was completed in 1949. The present arrangements emerged in a series of rapid steps or phases largely in response to the experience acquired in rural areas during the course of the reforms. The first phase consisted of a redistributive land reform.[1] During this phase, which occupied the early 1950s, perhaps as much as half the arable land was expropriated without compensation and turned over to poor peasants and other country folk with low incomes. This phase resulted in the creation of a system of small family farms.

This was not the end of the reform movement, however. From the very beginning the government and the communist party encouraged peasants to join together and form cooperative organizations.[2] Initially the institutions were very simple, even primitive, and consisted of little more than peasants pooling their labour, animals and implements to undertake agreed agricultural tasks. This was the phase of mutual aid teams.

The next phase included the formation of lower-level cooperatives. Under this arrangement members joined together to create a cooperative, but they retained title to their land and they received an income which reflected not only the amount of labour they contributed but also the amount of land they owned. By 1956, however, most of the lower-level cooperatives had evolved into higher-level cooperatives in which a member's income depended solely on the amount of work contributed. In this phase property titles were extinguished and payment was entirely according to work. By the end of this phase China had a socialist agricultural system.

The process did not stop here, however. The "Great Leap Forward" began immediately afterwards, in 1958, and during the next two years virtually the entire population of rural China was organized into very large communes in which an attempt was made to apply communist principles of production and distribution. Almost all forms of private property were abolished; communal dining, living and child rearing institutions were encouraged; material incentives were abandoned and a system of payment according to need was introduced.

This bold experiment failed. The rural economy was seriously disrupted and production fell sharply, partly because of bad weather but mostly because of ill considered policies. This abortive step revealed that any premature equalization (through one-step communization) of erstwhile villages would generate serious local level political dissensions, and would therefore damage the rural production system as well. Responding quickly, in 1960 the communes were reorganized along the lines that exist today.[3] Power was decentralized from the commune to the production team, some material incentives were restored, communist social institutions were abolished and an important but highly

---

1 The classic study of this phase is William Hinton, *Fanshen: A Documentary of Revolution in a Chinese Village*, Monthly Review Press, 1966.
2 The development of socialist agriculture in China can be seen in tabular form in A.L. Erisman, "China: Agricultural Development, 1949 – 71", Joint Economic Committee, U.S. Congress, *People's Republic of China: An Economic Assessment*, 18 May 1972, p. 117.
3 About 5 per cent of the land in China is organized as state farms. These tend to be in frontier areas or, if located elsewhere, are used as experimental farms.

circumscribed role was given to private production and marketing. Production quickly recovered and a unique system of socialist agriculture was firmly established in China.

The foundation of the system, as we have seen, is the production team, a group of neighbours consisting, say, of 50 households and more than 200 persons. The team is responsible for almost all crop production and most collective animal husbandry. The team usually is the level at which accounts are kept and it is at the team where the details of the work-point system of payment are determined. The next level up is the production brigade consisting, say, of 400 households and roughly 1,600 persons. The brigades are responsible for many industrial and sideline activities; they own pools of equipment and run repair shops. They also run primary schools and rural medical clinics. The commune of, say, 4,000 households and 16,000 persons may run a few relatively large industries; it is also likely to be responsible for fishing, forestry and some livestock activities. It is in charge of the system of health care and of secondary education although the state is now beginning to assume responsibility for the latter.

The People's Commune is a powerful instrument for fulfilling the growth and distributional objectives of rural development. Let us first note how it has contributed to the generation of economic growth. First, the commune system has proved to be an effective instrument for ensuring the full utilization of labour and land. Second, it has led to substantial improvement in the efficiency of resource allocation, e.g., through the elimination of some field boundaries and the consolidation of small plots into larger fields. It has also enabled Chinese agriculture to take advantage of some economies of scale associated with the use of tractors and harvesters. Third, by promoting a more diversified economy, it has reduced risk, with the possible consequence of increasing the propensity of the peasantry to innovate.

Fourth, the commune has been a remarkably successful vehicle for mobilizing seasonally unemployed labour for farm capital construction projects. Much of the development in rural China has originated from the efforts of commune labourers engaged in a wide variety of investment schemes organized by teams, brigades, communes and the county government. The commune in particular has been able to internalize the benefits of a great many rural investments and this is a major cause of its success. Fifthly, the commune also has been able to generate a large flow of savings in rural areas and to channel these into small scale industry. Such industry, in turn, has strengthened the commune's technical and financial capacity to mechanize agriculture, thus freeing more labour for infrastructural and industrial activities. Part of the surplus from rural industries is used to support welfare programmes such as schools and clinics, both of which tend to raise labour productivity in general. The integration of small scale industries within the commune also helps to reduce migration of agricultural workers into the towns. Additionally, the industrial skills which are acquired by the commune workforce are retained and employed within the commune itself. Thus, the dynamism of the Chinese countryside stems in large part from the ability of the commune system to ensure high rates of saving and capital accumulation. This is perhaps its outstanding characteristic from the point of view of generating rural development.

The private sector plays an important role within the commune system. Approximately 5 – 7 per cent of a commune's land is allocated to households for private cultivation. These tiny kitchen gardens not only supply the needs of the family for many fruits and vegetables, they also produce a marketable surplus which can be sold either in the village fairs, an unregulated market, or to the state. In addition, the household economy usually raises poultry and a few pigs, some of which are consumed and some sold. Lastly, the household economy may also engage in handicraft activities. Income from these private sources often appears to constitute 20 – 40 per cent of a household's total income.

The household sector makes a noticeable contribution to saving and investment in rural areas. Stocks of grain are accumulated in large volume by households. These inventories of foodgrains strengthen the collective's defence against famine and hunger and this form of investment appears to be the priority outlet for savings in rural areas. Next comes saving and investment in privately owned houses. In the great majority of communes the stock of dwellings is privately owned and additions to the stock are financed by household savings. On the whole the quality of housing compares favourably with that in other large Asian countries and the fact that this is so is testimony to the importance of the private sector.

The size of the private sector is carefully controlled. Households are not allowed to employ outside labour — that is considered to be exploitation — and hence the number of workers in a household's private economy is limited by the size of the family. Households have no opportunity to acquire capital equipment beyond such simple items as a sewing machine or bicycle. Hence the capital base of the household economy is limited. Equally, the amount of land that is made available to the private sector is severely restricted and consequently there is little danger that collective and private farming will be forced to compete for, say, labour. Finally, produce offered for sale in the private market must be sold by a member of the producing household and hence a specialist group of traders and other middlemen is not allowed to develop.

These policies are designed to prevent the household economy from growing too large and undermining collective economic activities. At the same time, the private sector is given a certain amount of freedom and within the rules of the system is even allowed to flourish. A remarkable thing about the private sector is that it is inserted into the collective sector in such a way that it reduces local inequality in the distribution of income. The reason for this is that the incentives to participate in the private economy are strongest for those households with an above average number of either very old or very young people. That is, the private sector is most attractive to people who for one reason or another are unable to play a full part in collective economic activities. Everything else being equal, households with many such people would tend to be relatively poor, but the availability of economic opportunities in the private sector gives them alternative sources of income and therefore reduces their poverty.

Recent policy has reaffirmed the legitimacy and extended the domain of household economic activities. It is recognized that the private sector supplements and is complementary to the collective economy. Indeed the household economy frequently uses scraps of land that otherwise would be idle for such things as raising bees, collecting medicinal herbs or growing bamboo. It requires little capital compared to collective activities. For example, collective piggeries or collective chicken or duck farms require allocations of animal feed, people to take care of the animals and the construction of appropriate structures. All of these things compete for resources with other collective activities. Private pig raising or chicken raising, on the other hand, uses resources from individual households and often these resources would otherwise be unutilized. That is, the opportunity cost of the resources used in the private sector is low. This is almost certainly true of labour, too.

The reason for this is that much of the labour that is devoted to the private sector would not otherwise be available to the collective sector; more likely it would have remained idle. This is exemplified by the case of private house building activity. Houses are built in the off-peak season, which explains why housing in the relatively dry Hebei Province was noticeably superior to that in Shanghai communes, even though the latter are financially far better off. The social opportunity cost of labour expended on private house construction was clearly far greater in the south. So also, bricks were produced in large quantities in the Shanghai communes, but were largely exported to the urban areas for State construction activity, rather than being retained for private house construction within the communes. Thus the existence of the household economy reduces leisure and increases the total amount of work done, rather than merely diverting labour from the collective to the private sector.

Within the collective economy recent policy has reaffirmed the primacy of the production team. This has implications for income distribution policy which we shall discuss below. It also has implications, however, for planning. Specifically, teams are to be given greater authority to make their own production plans, to take local conditions and preferences into account and to use greater initiative in searching for profitable income earning opportunities. The planning role of the production brigades will therefore be weakened, as will the planning role of the state as represented in the commune administration. Agricultural planning, in consequence, may become more "indicative", with fewer targets, quotas and "tasks" handed down by higher authorities, and more reliance being placed on planning via the market mechanism.

The institutional framework that has evolved in China and the planning system that has accompanied it have permitted rural development to occur at an acceptable if not spectacular rate. The pace of expansion has been uneven: agricultural growth was rapid until the late 1950s, but from then until the end of the 1960s it barely kept up with population growth; since 1970, however, the average rate of growth of agricultural output has been one and a half to two times as fast as the rate of growth of the population.

If one considers the 25 year period from 1952 to 1977, it appears that the output of grains — that is, rice, wheat, coarse grains and the grain equivalent of potatoes[4] — increased about 2.3 per cent a year.[5] The output of all food items increased faster still, although the lack of data makes it impossible to present accurate estimates. It is evident, however, that the production of grain increased less rapidly than the average and thus a time series of grain output is a misleading proxy for total food output. Non-food agricultural production expanded more rapidly than the output of food and, of course, faster than grain production alone. A reasonable estimate is that the gross value of total agricultural output grew about 2.9 per cent a year during 1952 – 77.

If one is interested not in agricultural production but in rural incomes, one must take into account the income generated in rural industrial and handicraft activities. Unfortunately, there are no reliable estimates of the rate of growth of rural industry, but it is clear from fragmentary evidence that it has been very rapid, probably faster than 20 per cent a year for the last quinquennium. The proportion of rural output originating in the industrial sector still is fairly low, although its importance is increasing year by year. Even during the period we are considering its contribution must have been sufficiently large to raise the rate of growth of total income in rural areas to well above 3 per cent a year. This is not a bad performance, especially when one takes into account the fact that China's population was growing only 2.1 per cent a year and its rural population only 1.8 per cent a year. The present rates of demographic increase are of course lower still.

At the end of February 1978 a Ten Year Plan (1976 – 85) was announced which required a sharp acceleration in the rate of growth of grain production of 3.5 per cent a year from 1976 (or 4.5 per cent from 1978) and a rate of growth of total agricultural production of nearly 5 per cent a year. These probably were excessively ambitious targets and they almost certainly will be revised downwards. It certainly should be possible, however, to achieve an annual rate of growth of grain production of 3 per cent or slightly more and of total agricultural production of 4 per cent. If, in addition, the rate of growth of population could be reduced to somewhere between 1.0 and 1.5 per cent a year, this would ensure a rapid increase in average rural income and constitute a remarkable achievement.

In 1979, however, the Ten Year Plan was set aside and a three year readjustment programme was introduced. The purpose of this programme is to eliminate several "imbalances" in the economy that are regarded as impeding further progress. These imbalances are between (a) investment and consumption, (b) heavy and light manufacturing and (c) agriculture and industry. Under the readjustment policy capital formation will be reduced and there will be a freeze on steel production and the output of machinery. It is hoped that this will

4 The conversion rate is four metric tons of potatoes to one metric ton of grain.
5 Data on growth rates are taken from Anthony M. Tang and Bruce Stone, *Food Production in the People's Republic of China*, IFPRI Research Report No. 15, Washington, May 1980.

release funds for agriculture and light industry as well as allow the level of consumption to rise.

Readjustment is to be accompanied by "restructuring". By this is meant a devolution of decision making power away from the centre to local units. The primary purpose of "restructuring" is not to increase grass-roots democracy but to encourage efficiency in resource utilization. In this way it is hoped that growth can be sustained despite the lower rate of investment.

The Distribution of Income and Wealth

There are many facets to the distribution of income and wealth. Perhaps the facet which ultimately is of greatest interest is the distribution among households, but in a socialist society one would also want to compare incomes among collective units. Similarly, in any society, inter-regional, inter-sectoral, and inter-class differences also require examination. We will touch upon the first two aspects of inequality to the extent that our evidence permits, although in the main, our concern will be with the intra-rural distribution of income. After forming an approximate idea of the spread of inequality at different levels, we will briefly discuss how institutional and other economic policies contribute to the redistributive objective.

In general terms, however, it is clear that the distribution of income and wealth among households in rural China is remarkably even. It is broadly comparable to the best that has been achieved in the capitalist countries and is much more equal than in the great majority of Third World countries. The most reliable figures at our disposal refer to distributed collective income and consequently we shall concentrate on these. Unfortunately, however, distributed collective income is only a partial measure of a household's total income because it excludes income originating in the private sector, and thus it is not an ideal measure. Further, when comparing collective units, this measure understates the extent of income inequality because it does not include collective savings in the reckoning. None the less, one can obtain a summary impression of the degree of equality by observing the narrowness of the range of distributed collective incomes.

In the province of Hebei, as we saw in Chapter 2, the range of per capita distributed collective income among counties was 1:4.78 in 1979. If the evidence from this large province can be regarded as typical of the other provinces of China, it would appear that the most prosperous county of a province is likely to be about five times richer than the poorest. Differences among communes within a county are negligible. For example, in 1978 the richest commune in Jia Ding county was 37 per cent better off than the poorest; in Shanghai county and Fo Gang county the percentages were 40 and 48, respectively. Thus, within a county it is reasonable to suppose that an upper estimate of the range of commune per capita income is roughly 1:1.5. That is, the richest commune normally would not be more than about 50 per cent more prosperous than the poorest.

Let us now consider the range of income per head among brigades of a commune. The highest degree of inequality we observed was in Wu Gong Commune, Hebei where in 1978 the richest brigade was 2.85 times richer than the poorest. However, in Qie Ma Commune, Hebei and in Tang Tang Commune, Guangdong the range was 1:1.52 and 1:1.61, respectively, in the same year. Similarly, in Evergreen People's Commune, Beijing Municipality the per capita income of the richest brigade was only 51 per cent greater than that of the poorest brigade in 1976. Hence it would appear that within a commune the range of brigade incomes tends to be about 1:2 or less.

The data presented in Chapter 3 indicate that variations in income per head at the team level on occasion can be substantial. For example, in Xin Tang Brigade of Tang Tang Commune the range of incomes among the 19 teams is 1:4.95. This is misleading, however, because the teams which were poorest in terms of distributed collective income were also the teams which benefited disproportionately from incomes earned off the commune in state owned factories. Once outside employment in the state sector is taken into account, the ratio of highest to lowest per capita team income falls to 3.25. Even this appears to be an unusually wide range, moreover. Considering the whole of Wu Gong Commune, not just a brigade, the richest of the 36 teams was only a bit more than three times more prosperous than the poorest; in Cheng Dong Commune the richest of the 141 teams was significantly less than three times as prosperous as the poorest team. Indeed, inspection of our evidence suggests that within a brigade the range of per capita team incomes typically is about 1:1.5.

One might be tempted to use these highly stylized facts to build up a picture of the overall distribution of distributed collective income per head. One possible way to do this would be to take the extremes of the distribution at each level, i.e. the range of incomes, and multiply them together. For example, if the richest team of a brigade is 1.5 times richer than the poorest, and the richest brigade of a commune is 2 times richer than the poorest, one might be inclined to argue that the richest team of a commune would be about 3 times (1.5×2) richer than the poorest. Continuing this procedure all the way to province level, our stylized facts might lead one to believe that within a province the per capita distributed collective income of the richest team is about 22.5 times higher than that of the poorest team ($1.5 \times 2 \times 1.5 \times 5 = 22.5$).

This procedure is very misleading, however. First of all, it focuses only on the extremes of the distribution, whereas in fact most observations are clustered close to the average. Second, implicit in the use of this procedure is the assumption that the observed range of sub-unit inequality applies to all such units, i.e., that if the range of, say, brigade incomes within a commune is 1:2, this is true of all communes irrespective of their position in the inter-commune income profile. The data that we report on the range of inequality at different levels of the rural collective economy is derived from units which, in fact, were situated close to the average applicable to those levels. But it is possible that the range of inequality might be more restricted at the poorer end on account of the operation of policies which underwrite a moderate minimum floor level. So also the range might have been eroded at the top end as well through the operation of such redistributive policies and mechanisms which are linked to the growth process itself. There is indeed some evidence of the operation of both these effects. It is conceivable, then, that the units clustered close to the average might display a wider range of inequality than that applicable at the two ends of the spectrum. In this case, the effect of the multiplicative procedure is greatly to exaggerate the differences in income between the poorest and richest teams at the provincial level. In fact, the multiplication procedure indicates the maximum possible range of team incomes within a province. The actual range will always be much smaller than this.

Fortunately, in Chapter 2 we were able to present data on per capita distributed collective income for all the teams of two provinces, namely, Hebei and Guangdong. These data[6] indicate that in both provinces the range of team income is approximately 1:10. This range is less than half as wide as the multiplication procedure suggests and illustrates clearly the dangers of constructing a macro-economic picture from fragmentary micro-economic sources. Even so, it is evident that inter-team inequality at the provincial level is of some significance. Furthermore, when we examine data on income differences between provinces it will become apparent that in the nation as a whole the degree of rural inequality is greater still.

Thus, the inter-regional income range is approximately 1:2 (though it should be noted that the inter-regional range of rural incomes alone is likely to be somewhat less). At the other end of the inequality tree, the range of per capita household incomes within a team is also roughly 1:2. Again using the multiplicative method, a range of 1:40 could be generated at the household level for the country as a whole. For the reasons stated earlier, this is likely to be an overestimate; a more realistic figure might be nearer 1:25, excluding the extreme observations at either end. This implies a moderate level of inequality in the context of a socialist economy, and emphasizes the uneven level of development of different regions of China. It should be noted, however, that a similar comparison based on consumption (especially foodgrains) would narrow the range very sharply on account of the high floor level underwritten by the provisions of "the five guarantees". Viewed in this manner, it can be argued that these differences are modest by the standards of the majority of underdeveloped countries.

Confirmation of this is provided by statistics[7] compiled by the Chinese for the summer of 1980, relating to the approximately 5.04 million rural accounting units throughout the country. The per capita average income — presumably collective — of 27.3 per cent of the units was found to be below 50 yuan. The percentage of units with average incomes between 50 and 100 yuan, and more than 100 yuan, was found to be approximately 50 per cent and slightly less than 25 per cent, respectively. About 12 per cent of the rural population con-

6   See Tables 2:2 and 2:3 of Chapter 2.
7   BBC Summary of World Broadcasts: 8 Nov. 1980, FE/6570/C1/2; based on an article by Wu Xiang in the *People's Daily*, 5 Nov. 1980.

stantly "relied on resold grain for their food supply, loans for production and subsidies for day-to-day living." This last statistic provides us with a rough idea of the dimensions of poverty from the production, or income generation point of view, but overstates the proportion of the rural population who failed to have their basic needs met through either the production or redistributive channels. Without wishing to sound complacent about the slow rate of increase of rural incomes (as against production) during the 1960s and early 1970s, and without underestimating the potential for further redistributive measures, it must nevertheless be emphasized that impressive ground has been gained already on meeting the distributional objectives of development.

We can now turn to a brief review of the range of institutional and other economic policies which have a bearing upon the intra-rural distribution of income. The most dramatic improvement in the distribution of income in rural China occurred during the period of land confiscation and redistribution in 1949 – 52. It was not until 1956, however, that private ownership of the means of production was abolished and consequently it was only then that most of the major differences in the distribution of wealth in the countryside disappeared. The subsequent collectivization of agriculture has helped to consolidate the improvement in the distribution of income that was achieved during the revolutionary land redistribution period. It has also ensured that local inequalities in the distribution of wealth will not exceed a modest level. Today, rural people own their own homes, a range of consumer durables, a few animals and some simple implements; in addition, they possess a store of grain and a small bank account. All of this leads to some inequality in the distribution of wealth, but the differences are not very great.

Let us first consider the policies governing inter-household income differentials. It was argued earlier in Chapter 3 that the demographic characteristics of households form the primary source of income inequality at this level. Within the institutional framework of the rural commune, several forces, or policies, have contributed directly or indirectly, to a reduction in the level of such inequality. Firstly, between 50 and 80 per cent of the grain distribution within a production team is made on the basis of the size of the households, i.e., according to the "need" criterion. This implies that the income differentials generated by differences in the dependency ratios across households are severely circumscribed. Secondly, the provision of "the five guarantees"[8] provides a moderate income floor to the poorest, labour-short households, thereby narrowing differentials further. Thirdly, until the recent attacks on the "Learn from Dazhai" campaign, the Dazhai system[9] of work measurement was extensively practised. This system was "egalitarian" in that it tended to compress the range across which daily work-points could be earned. Fourthly, as was argued earlier, the household's private economic activities tend to reduce inter-house-

8 Food, clothing, fuel, school fees and burial expenses. Subsequently, a sixth "guarantee", medical cover, was added to the list.
9 For a detailed discussion, see Neville Maxwell, "The Tachai Way" in Neville Maxwell, ed., *China's Road to Development*, Pergamon Press, 1979, pp. 41 – 96.

hold differences because such income is related to the labour input of the dependents in a household.

These policies tend to narrow inter-household income differences within a production team. In addition, there are other powerful mechanisms inherent within the institution of the commune which reduce intra-commune inequalities at the inter-brigade and inter-team levels. For convenience of exposition such mechanisms, or policies, can be grouped into four categories.

Firstly, the commune and the brigade undertake substantial investments in the development of the infrastructure of the units concerned. This might consist of such things as road construction (which reaches out to the less accessible units), extension of irrigation and water control facilities to the hitherto dry areas, and other forms of farm capital construction. Since these and similar activities tend inevitably to involve the poorer units, such outlays tend to be equalizing in nature. Secondly, there are other policies which appear, *prima facie*, to be "neutral" but in fact are redistributive by virtue of distributing expenditure on commune or brigade level facilities on a per capita, proportional basis. One example of this is provided by the communal welfare facilities available to all members of the commune. Thus, access to education and medical care is not linked to household or team income, and hence expenditure on these services tends to reduce overall inequalities between otherwise differentiated units. Indeed, poorer units might make greater use of medical services and thereby accentuate the equalizing effect. Another illustration is provided by the general practice followed by commune and brigade enterprises of allocating their highly prized jobs among units on a proportional basis, i.e., according to the proportion that the labour force of the units concerned forms of the total labour force of the commune. The equalizing impact of such a policy is accentuated and reaches individual poor households of the lower units when, as sometimes happens, the enterprises pay wages not to the workers but to the teams from which the workers come.

The third category of policies relates to those which discriminate directly in favour of the poorer units. These are explicitly redistributive. Again, such policies can be of several types. For example, the enterprise jobs mentioned above were found on occasion to be allocated preferentially to the poorer teams. Where brigade or commune machines are required by the team for agricultural work, these can be made available to the poorer teams without cost, or on a preferential basis. Poor units frequently receive grants or loans of money from higher levels within the commune. Where a team or brigade encounters management problems, higher level cadres can be stationed with the unit to help to overcome its weaknesses. Redistributive policies such as these can be implemented by the county as well, although in most instances they are intra-commune in nature.

The fourth category consists of the unique method of equalizing the incomes of, say, various teams through the device of raising the unit of accounting from the team-level to the brigade-level. This has the immediate effect of pooling together the resources of all the teams of the brigade concerned, i.e., land, machines, labour, etc., and thereby equalizing the value of the workday across teams. Accounting at the level of the commune was attempted during the period of the "Great Leap Forward". As we know, this ambitious experiment failed. In principle, however, commune level accounting would have the effect of equalizing access of all members to the pooled resources of the constituent units. Moreover, such a measure would internalize a wide range of technical, organizational and pecuniary external economies and would thereby contribute to growth as well. But the most important thing about commune level accounting is that it is the most powerful equalizing instrument available to the commune.

We will have more to say on this point later. For the moment we need only note that this method for achieving greater equality has not been widely used in rural China. Indeed, commune level accounting is rarely used even in areas where the commune has satisfied all the conditions that must be met before the level of accounts is raised. Perhaps the explanation for this is that the bitter lessons of the early failed experiments have been remembered a bit too vividly.

Quite independently of the operation of the above four sets of policy-based measures, there is a process endogenous to the commune system which tends to produce greater equality in the medium and long runs, viz., a tendency for the aggregate productivity of resources to decline on the margin with an increase in the development of the unit. This has been analysed in detail in Chapter 5 and we will not dwell upon it here. It should be remembered, however, that this tendency is offset to some extent by a disequalizing tendency that arises from the observed fact that the ratio of collective accumulation to net income is positively associated with the level of per capita net income of the collective unit. As a result, rich units, with their higher propensity to accumulate, could grow more rapidly than poor unless either the poor received capital transfers to help them increase their rate of accumulation or unless the tendency for marginal aggregate productivity to decline in rich units completely offset their advantages in the domain of investment.

The full range of the policies enumerated above has operated in rural China, although they have not been applied uniformly by region or continuously in time. Even so, the degree of equality that has been achieved can be attributed to the systematic application of such measures. Equally, the observed moderate levels of inequality can be viewed as an indication of the actual, if not potential, limits of such policies. Perhaps a more persuasive argument would be that the policies commonly used need more time to reduce the presently observed inequalities to insignificant levels. Such evidence as is available suggests that there has been a tendency over time for intra-rural inequalities at the local level to decline. It is important, therefore, to investigate, even if only sketchily, whether the new set of policies will narrow or widen existing inequalities in rural China. We will offer some tentative ideas on this issue at both the household and collective levels in turn.

At the household level, it would appear that the new policies are likely to widen differences among households. First, the proportion of the grain output being allocated according to the need criterion is being reduced and there is a correspondingly higher proportion being allocated according to work. This step is, of course, compatible with the socialist rules of distribution and it has been introduced explicitly in order to increase work incentives in the countryside. There are also reports, second, that a tougher attitude is to be taken than before on the question of the repayment of the deficits of poor households. An interest charge is to be made against outstanding cash deficits and households are in general to be required to repay loans even of long standing. Since such loans generally are made to the poorer households, this policy, to the extent that it is implemented, is likely to increase household differences.

Thirdly, the Dazhai system of workpoint estimation has been given up, and in its place have been introduced a variety of alternative systems, all of which are designed to emphasize work incentives. The effect of these new payment systems will be to widen the gap between the labour abundant and the labour poor households. Lastly, it could be argued that the widening of the domain of private activities at the household level is likely, according to our earlier results, to be equalizing in nature. To some extent this probably will be so. However, it is now possible for rich households to use their savings to purchase a machine to use in producing household level goods for sale in the free market. In other words, whereas previously private income was related almost exclusively to the availability of labour, it could now become increasingly possible for a household to compensate for its shortage of labour (provided by children and old persons) through the use of more capital intensive methods. Of course, no commune member can hire workers to supply labour in the household's activities, but within this constraint, rich households could begin to gain at least as much as the poorer households from private economic activities.

At the level of the collective units, there are no additional policies designed for the reduction of inequality. On the other hand, there is an increasingly clear policy stance on two of the equalizing measures mentioned earlier. First, it is no longer the policy to encourage collective units to raise their accounting level when they have met the conditions previously established for doing so. On the contrary, it is now the policy to freeze the present level of accounts, and even to revert to lower accounting levels. This has taken the form of breaking up production teams into semi-permanent work groups, and in certain border regions of breaking up the team into individual household economic units. It is also the view that brigade or commune level accounting units should revert to lower levels of account unless conditions are highly favourable for continuing at the same level. Second, the earlier policy of preferential loans and grants in favour of the poorer teams or brigades appears to have been terminated in practice, on the grounds that such assistance generates dependence upon external assistance for development, encourages or permits bad management, etc.

In addition, there is now a policy to replace the earlier workpoint system of payment in commune and brigade enterprises with fixed cash wages. Formerly, the payment could be made to the team from which the worker was drawn, whereas it is now to be made directly to the worker. Very often, this new system has the effect of widening the wage gap between the commune's agricultural and industrial workers.

In general, the new attitude appears to be against redistributive measures at the local level, and indeed explicitly condones substantial income inequalities on the argument that poor households would work more if they could see their neighbours becoming prosperous. In fact, it is openly recognized by the new regime that income inequalities are likely to widen as a result of its economic policies. We shall return to this topic later.

Regional Inequality

It is less clear what has been happening to regional inequalities. We know that regional income disparities were quite wide in the 1950s. Some scholars believe, however, that "available data seem to indicate that these disparities were diminishing, even if only quite gradually, between 1952, 1957 and 1971."[10] It is possible that these disparities declined further during the 1970s, but if so it is probably because, as a result of policy, state "industry in backward areas, it seems, has grown faster than the national average ... ."[11] Thus differences in regional per capita industrial income may have declined.

In agriculture, however, the poorer regions may have grown less rapidly than the national average. This, at least, seems to have happened in the province of Szechuan between 1957 and 1976.[12] If Szechuan is typical it is likely that differences in regional per capita agricultural income increased in recent years. Disparities in rural incomes may either have increased or diminished depending on whether or not the relative expansion of rural industry in poor regions offset the relative decline of agricultural output. But, given the very low proportion that industrial income forms of all income in the backward regions, their industrial growth rates would have had to be spectacularly high to be able to compensate for their relative sluggishness in agricultural growth in comparison with the more advanced regions.

In fact, we cannot even be sure of how large is the range in regional per capita rural income. Recent estimates by Bruce Stone, however, make it possible to guess.

Let us use as a proxy for rural income per head, average foodgrain distribution per capita. This almost certainly understates inequality since grains are likely to be distributed more equally than income as a whole. Next, let us assume that Xinjiang Uighur Autonomous Region is one of the poorest if not the poor-

10 Alexander Eckstein, *China's Economic Revolution*, Cambridge University Press, 1977, p. 304. See also Nicholas Lardy, *Economic Growth and Distribution in China*, Cambridge University Press, 1978.
11 Nick Eberstadt, *Poverty in China*, International Development Institute, Indiana University, 1979, p. 25.
12 Private communication from Nicholas Lardy of Yale University.

est region in China. This is a plausible assumption. Xinjiang is China's largest regional administrative unit and covers a vast area in northwestern China between the USSR and Tibet. It is a remote and inhospitable region consisting of high mountains, deserts, arid basins and grasslands. Finally, let us assume that Jiangsu province is the richest region in China. This, too, is a plausible assumption. Jiangsu is the most densely populated province of China (and includes the independent municipality of Shanghai); it occupies a well-watered alluvial plain and enjoys the highest output per unit of land of any province in the country.

In 1978 average foodgrain distribution per capita was 184.8 kilograms in Xinjiang and 249.5 in Jiangsu.[13] This is a difference of 35 per cent. In 1977, the figures for Xinjiang and Jiangsu were 169.3 and 219.5 kg., respectively, a difference of 29.7 per cent.[14] The question now is by how much should one adjust these figures in order to obtain a reasonable guess as to the order of magnitude of regional inequalities?

Sample survey data of households in India suggest that individuals consuming the amount of grain characteristic of Xinjiang would allocate about 63 per cent of their total expenditure on foodgrains, whereas individuals consuming at the level characteristic of Jiangsu would spend about 50 per cent of their total income on foodgrains.[15] If one assumes away the effects of differing tastes, relative prices, etc., and applies these percentages to the Chinese data assembled by Bruce Stone, it follows that total income per head in Jiangsu is about 1.7 times that in Xinjiang. Two qualifications must be made about this estimate, however.

First, in using provinces and autonomous regions as our units of observation, we are in effect using political and administrative criteria to delineate regions. Yet there is no reason to believe that economic regions are correctly described by political boundaries. On the contrary, it is possible, even likely, that many provinces contain several regions and consequently differences in provincial averages understate differences in regional incomes when regions are properly defined. Secondly, we have excluded from our observations the rural areas included within the Beijing, Shanghai and Tientsin municipalities, yet communes in these municipalities probably are even more prosperous than the communes in a rich province such as Jiangsu. Indeed, it is arguable that households in the rural communes of Shanghai municipality are the richest peasant households in China and most of them are more prosperous than households in urban areas dependent upon industrial employment. By excluding these households, once again we understate regional inequality. Further adjustments to our estimates in order to correct these biases are bound to be arbitrary. Our best guess, nevertheless, is that the range of regional inequality is likely to be of the order of 1:2.

---

13 Bruce Stone, *A Review of Chinese Agricultural Statistics, 1949 – 79*, IFPRI Research Report No. 16, Washington (forthcoming), cited in A.M. Tang and B. Stone, *op. cit.*, Table 3, p. 95.
14 *Ibid.*
15 See V.M. Dandekar and N. Rath, *Poverty in India*, Ch. 1, Economic and Political Weekly, Bombay, 1971.

An important issue is whether policies at the regional level are tending to increase or diminish these inequalities. The first principle of regional policy has always been provincial or local self-help, if not self-sufficiency at a rudimentary level. However, under the cover of this wide umbrella, several specific regional policies have operated over time. In order to reach a judgement on this issue, moreover, one must consider not only the effects of direct regional policies but also the impact on regional differentials of a series of other economic policies.

Nicholas Lardy has argued that the budgetary operations of the central government have had an implicit redistributive bias.[16] Throughout the 1950s and probably the 1960s as well, the richer provinces were remitting a significant proportion of their revenues to the central government, whereas the poorer provinces were drawing substantial subsidies from the centre. This is taken as evidence of a transfer of resources from rich to poor regions. There are two problems with this interpretation, however. First, it is not possible to confirm the presence of such an effect in the 1970s. Second, the evidence itself is inconclusive because it does not take into account the distribution of the burden of the pricing policies which produced the revenue surpluses in the rich provinces. On the other hand, it is plausible to assume that the vast proportion of the value of output generated in the rich regions was bought or paid for by the residents of the rich regions. Thus, on balance, it must also be the case that the burden of generating the surpluses is borne by the rich regions themselves and hence the nominal transfer would represent a real transfer.

In the industrial sector, there has been a long standing policy of giving special preference to backward regions in deciding on the location of major new industrial ventures. However, the emphasis placed upon this measure may be reduced in future because of the overriding concern of the government with increasing the cost efficiency of new industrial enterprises.

Within the industrial sector, the new policies have favoured light industries, especially those at commune level. Commune level enterprises are now exempt from taxation until the profit rate becomes 3,000 yuan a year. The previous level of exemption was 600 yuan a year, and thus the change represents a substantial improvement from the point of view of the commune. Moreover, in the autonomous regions and in counties located on the frontiers of the country, all rural industries except cotton mills, tobacco factories, distilleries and wineries are exempt from taxation for five years regardless of the level of profits. The latter measure, though not the former, is bound to reduce regional inequality. But in view of the rather poor level of development of the commune industrial sector in the backward regions, the quantitative impact of this measure is likely to be modest. It is questionable whether such measures are strong enough to overcome the disadvantages of location in an industrially and agriculturally backward province or region. Commune and brigade industries have in fact been developing at a faster pace in the industrially advanced regions

16 Nicholas Lardy, *op. cit.*

and it is unlikely that a general policy of tax reliefs will alter the high and perhaps growing inequality in the spatial distribution of the commune industrial sector.

While the regional implications of fiscal and industrial policies are not insignificant, answers to the most important regional questions are perhaps to be found in the policies influencing the behaviour of the agricultural sector. It can be argued that the great effort to promote rural development with labour intensive methods during the 1950s must have reduced regional differentials. Within the context of the traditional technological framework, self-reliance and self-help would have contributed to this. However, with the arrival of the new bio-chemical inputs into agriculture in the 1960s, it is likely that the balance would have shifted strongly in favour of the already developed regions which possessed efficient water management systems and fertile soils. This widening tendency would have been accentuated by the longstanding policy of favourable treatment, with regard to resource allocation, of the marketable grain base areas, which in general tended to coincide with the areas of "stable and high yields". In order to obtain a more accurate idea of the likely future course of regional agricultural disparities, it is necessary to review a wide range of economic policies.

(i) Regional Specialization

Two points need to be noted here. The first concerns the reversal of the earlier policy of encouraging (or of requiring) all regions to attempt to be self-sufficient in grains, even if this meant forgoing the production of commercial crops for which the natural conditions were better suited. Regions have now been encouraged to choose their cropping pattern exclusively on the basis of economic criteria. Indeed, the rate of growth of output of the two most important commercial crops, viz., oilseeds and sugarcane, has outstripped that for foodgrains in the last two years. It is not obvious, however, that this is the result of a shift in the cultivated area away from grain to these crops. If so, it means the impressive increase in grain output is all the more remarkable. At present, a policy of providing incentives for the cultivation of commercial crops, even in grain deficit regions, is beginning to be implemented. From the vantage point of regional disparities, the new policy will improve the relative position of regions which though highly suited for the cultivation of commercial crops were nevertheless previously required to produce grain.

This is not to say that grain production is being ignored. A second feature of the specialization policy is to give even greater importance than before to the marketable grain base areas. Thus the traditional grain base areas and the newly designated industrial crop base areas are now singled out for special treatment.

(ii) Development Outlays

Regional disparities are directly affected by the central government's developmental expenditure in the agricultural sector. Agriculture, moreover, is now receiving higher priority than previously in the central plan and hence the importance of investment allocation is likely to increase. Modernization of the sector will focus on rural electrification, fertilizers, mechanization and irrigation and drainage works. The total expenditure on agricultural development, not including the element of subsidies to inputs and product prices, rose from 12.81 billion yuan in 1979 to 16.80 billion yuan in 1980, despite a drop in total plan expenditure from 120.30 to 114.29 billion yuan. Agriculture's share thus rose from 10.65 per cent to 14.70 per cent and it is expected to rise further in the near future. Within this total, the allocation for agricultural communes and their projects has declined somewhat, while the allocation under the category of capital construction projects has risen sharply. Much of this investment is in irrigation and will be located in drought prone areas. This policy will lead to higher output and incomes in economically backward areas and thus will tend to reduce regional inequalities. Moreover, since water and fertilizer are complementary inputs, investment in irrigation will raise the marginal product of chemical fertilizer and this should induce the planners to designate the areas benefiting from such investment as a grain or industrial crop "base" and allocate modern inputs to them. This is roughly the manner in which the strategy of expanding the areas of "high and stable yields" has operated. Illustrations of this policy are provided by the plans for opening up for cultivation 13 million hectares of wasteland, and also for the development of grasslands, in the northeast and northwest. Both these programmes should be finished by 1985, and should benefit relatively poor, sparsely populated regions.

Thus, apart from raising the rate of growth of agricultural output and dampening fluctuations, China's selective regional development strategy also reduces some regional differentials by incorporating hitherto underdeveloped areas into the regions of "high and stable yields". On the other hand, the same strategy has the effect of widening the income differentials between developed areas (including the recently developed ones) and the remaining underdeveloped regions. This is a consequence of favouring the developed regions in the allocation of bio-chemical inputs and other investment goods. The remaining regions, comprising most of the country, will be urged to practice self-reliance and to continue to advance by using traditional inputs more intensively and mobilizing their labour force for capital construction projects. The difficulty with this regional strategy is that both the grain and industrial crop "bases" tend to be in regions which already enjoy relatively high yields and incomes. A concentration of additional modern inputs in those areas is likely, therefore, on balance to increase regional income inequalities. Moreover, these regions may be prosperous at least in part because they already benefit from a disproportionate share of the modern inputs. It is possible, indeed, that diminishing returns to modern inputs may be present, and if so, the marginal product of some inputs (e.g. chemical fertilizer) may actually be higher outside the "bases" than inside them. If this turns out in practice to be the case, then regional policy not only would lead to greater inequality, it also would lead to greater inefficiency from the point of view of maximising aggregate output.

Overall, central developmental outlays in the agricultural sector are likely to favour regions which already are developed, or which are on the extensive margin of development, at the expense of regions which are undeveloped and which also are difficult to develop quickly. Spatial differences are bound to diminish in the long run, but in the short and medium terms it is likely that they will tend to increase.

(iii) Pricing Policies

A widening of regional differences in income is likely to be accentuated significantly by the new pricing policies for agricultural inputs and outputs. Agricultural inputs carry a substantial subsidy which obviously will benefit those regions which have better access to the inputs. Thus, the advanced regions gain not only from a superior access to the physical resources but also from being able to buy them cheaply.

State purchase prices for 18 major agricultural commodities recently have been raised substantially. For example, the quota sale price of grain has been raised by 20 per cent, the above-quota purchase price by 50 per cent and the negotiated purchases prices by anything up to 100 per cent. Undoubtedly such price increases raise the incomes of the peasantry. It is equally clear, however, that the new three tier price structure will channel most of the income gains to those advanced marketable grain base and industrial crop base areas which have large above-quota sales. Pricing policies, therefore, are likely to increase regional income differentials significantly. On the other hand, many poor areas are now exempt from compulsory state purchases. (Newly reclaimed land, too, is exempt from compulsory deliveries of grain for the first five years after it has entered production.) Such an exemption does not, however, represent a net gain. Under the previous policy, grain deficit regions which nevertheless were making quota sales to the State would have been able to buy back grain to meet their basic requirements at the quota price. Thus it might appear that exemption from quota sales would represent merely a neutral and administratively desirable measure. Now, however, grain deficit poor agricultural regions may find that they have to buy back grain from the State at the new quota purchase prices. This would represent a net loss, in absolute terms, for grain and income deficient regions.

(iv) Direct Poverty Relief

There are two measures that come under this heading. First, the 1980 budget "for the first time provides such development funds to boost production mainly in the old revolutionary base areas, remote border areas, autonomous localities inhabited by minorities and places with a comparatively poor economic foundation".[17] However, this assistance is quantitatively insignificant since it is at present only 500 million yuan.

---

17 Report by the Finance Minister Wang Bingqian to the Fifth PRC National People's Congress, August 30, 1980; Summary of World Broadcasts (SWB), FE/6525/C/1.

Second, a large number of poor production teams in backward regions have had their agricultural tax liabilities waived. Thus, in the fiscal year ending in March 1980, the central government remitted taxes worth 746 million yuan, or about 18 per cent of the total value of China's agricultural taxes. However, agricultural taxes form only about 4 per cent of the total value of agricultural output, and hence the remission amounts to no more than three-fourths of one per cent of this total value, hardly a significant sum. Even so, from the point of view of a production team, such a waiver represents funds which might have a very high opportunity cost. Thus, about 3300 production teams in Shandong Province were exempted from 1.91 million yuan in taxes in the past year. This is equivalent to about three or four yuan per capita, although the money was not distributed to households but was used to expand small industrial enterprises and side-line occupations and to diversify the rural economy. As a result, income increased by about 6 million yuan, or three times the amount of tax remitted. Further, as from April 1979, agricultural taxes are to be remitted for three consecutive years for "China's poorest production teams".[18] These measures, however, desirable as they are, are too small to make a serious impression on the extent of regional disparities.

(v) Private Activity and Spatial Distribution

The policies we have discussed so far affect primarily the collective and state sectors. There is also the question, however, of the effect of private economic activities on regional differences in income and wealth. Unfortunately, because of lack of information, our thoughts on this subject must be regarded as highly tentative, more in the nature of hypotheses than facts.

In the section in which we discussed the institutional framework for rural development, it was argued that the existence of the household economy tends to reduce inequality in the distribution of income within a particular commune. It does not necessarily follow from this, however, that the private sector is equalizing within a national context. Many informed observers undoubtedly believe that for the rural sector as a whole private income is distributed far less equally than collective income. The reason for this is that opportunities to earn large private sector incomes are very unequally distributed. Specifically, communes located near the relatively prosperous urban areas can supplement their collective income with revenue from private sales to city dwellers of vegetables, other farm produce and handicraft items. Communes such as those in the Shanghai Municipality are very favourably placed to reap large private sector incomes. Similar opportunities are unlikely to arise in communes less favourably situated, such as Tang Tang located in a less accessible region of Guangdong Province.

Casual observation on our own field trip does indeed indicate that private sector incomes are substantially higher in communes located on the

18 New China News Agency (NCNA), 3 July 1980; SWB, FE/W1096/A/6.

periphery of metropolitan areas than elsewhere. It is not at all unusual for a family in Cheng Dong Commune to earn 500 yuan or more in the private sector, and this is two or three times as much as families were earning in the private sector in the other communes we visited.

On the other hand, it is not enough to show that private sector incomes are absolutely larger in rich communes than in poor; one must show that private sector incomes are a higher proportion of total household income in rich communes than in poor. While this is difficult to establish conclusively with the data available, two pieces of evidence throw some light on the issue. The Oxford Rural China Delegation which studied communes in Suzhou Municipality in Jiangsu Province in June 1980 found that about 30 – 40 per cent of the peasants' incomes in this prime agricultural region was derived from private economic activities. The average distributed per capita income in the commune in question was in the neighbourhood of 200 yuan per year. In contrast, on the basis of data gathered by a major national survey, the Chinese State Statistical Bureau has estimated that private income constitutes about 17 per cent of rural per capita income. These two figures together are consistent with the hypothesis that private sector economic activities at the household level tend to widen regional differentials. This is not to deny the fact that within reasonable constraints and under supervision, the household's private sector can form a useful adjunct to the collective economy in its current stage of development.

(vi) De-collectivization

There is no doubt that the present government in China believes the private sector can make an important contribution toward raising living standards in rural China in general, but especially in the economically backward areas. This faith underpins several measures which have simultaneously extended the domain of the private sector while also enforcing a certain degree of de-collectivization. Thus, while household economic activities and rural trade fairs are being encouraged in general, and collective piggeries are being widely de-collectivized, more radical measures are being introduced in the poorer and border regions. The most important new measure is the increase in the size of the private plot. In Xinjiang, private plots are being doubled in size and in Tibet, too, they are to be enlarged, but not by so much. As a result of these changes, it might well turn out that private sector income soon will exceed income derived from the collective sector in several regions. However, this in itself does not imply that the private sector performs an equalizing role, since the resources which are transferred to private activities could have a significant opportunity cost in the collective sector.

Parallel to the increase in the private sector is a tendency in the developed areas for production contracts to be made with work groups. In the poorer regions there are signs that the production team is beginning to play a secondary role to the household economy and production contracts are being made directly with individual households. In other areas, there are reports that the production team is being replaced by the Mutual Aid Teams of old.

The stated purpose behind the moves to enlarge the role of the household economy in the backward regions is to reduce poverty. The logic implicit in the measures adopted is that by "bringing the enthusiasm of the masses into full play", by providing incentives to individual households, rural development will be accelerated. It can be argued, however, that this is rather optimistic. It is more likely, perhaps, that such measures will accentuate intra-regional inequalities at the household level while leaving inter-regional differences to go their own way.

Rural-Urban Inequality

Another important aspect of inequality is differences between rural and urban areas. In the 1950s per capita income in the cities was about twice that in the countryside. This is a considerable difference, although it is not as great as in the majority of Third World countries. Moreover, while it may well be true "that there are no clear signs it is diminishing",[19] the weight of evidence suggests that rural-urban inequality is less today than it was 25 years ago and, furthermore, recent policy changes are likely to result in a significant reduction in inequality in future.

We know that the terms of trade have moved sharply in favour of agriculture since 1963. The improvement was particularly great in 1979 when, as we have seen, the procurement price of grain delivered under quota was raised 20 per cent, the price of above quota grain was increased 50 – 100 per cent and the prices of agricultural inputs acquired from industry were reduced by 10 – 15 per cent. We also know that real wages in urban industry increased only marginally after 1957 during a period when per capita income in rural areas rose significantly, especially after the recovery from the Great Leap Forward. These movements in the terms of trade and in urban wages almost certainly led to some compression in rural-urban income differentials. The shift of policy after 1978 against heavy industry and in favour of light manufacturing, rural industries and agriculture is likely to lead to a further compression in rural-urban differentials in the years to come.

On the other hand, wages of 40 per cent of the workers in urban areas have been raised substantially as part of the new policy package, and furthermore, the wage packets of all state workers have been protected against the recent rises in food prices. Therefore, in order to get a more accurate impression, we need to look at the urban sector in relation not to an aggregated rural sector, but in relation to the developed and underdeveloped regions separately. The advanced rural areas almost certainly have gained even more than the urban areas from the new policy package. The underdeveloped rural regions, in contrast, probably have gained the least and have fallen behind in relation to the urban as well as the advanced rural areas.

Rural-urban differentials are widely perceived in the countryside. A

---

19 Nick Eberstadt, *op. cit.*, p. 24.

recent report from Hubei Province sums up some peasant objections to policies which exclude them from entering the more lucrative avenues of employment. In specific terms, four policies are singled out for criticism.

> (1) Recruitment of the labour force. The peasants are excluded from this. The present policy stipulates that when the State recruits workers, only those who eat 'commodity grain' are wanted, while those from the rural areas are not included.
> (2) Recruitment of PLA soldiers. There is a new policy this year. More soldiers are to be recruited from cities and towns.
> (3)Promotion of cadres. At present, cadres are not directly promoted from the ranks of workers, peasants and soldiers with a low educational level.
> (4) Admission of students. When the universities and post-secondary colleges enroll students, because the quality of education in the countryside is inferior, the ratio of students admitted is lower than in the cities … . Children of peasants find it very difficult to gain admission to schools.[20]

In summary, virtually all of the policies we have discussed, e.g., commodity pricing policy, agricultural input allocation policy, investment policy, land development programmes, tax policy and grain procurement policy, will contribute toward a reduction in the differences in income between rural and urban areas. Within the rural areas, however, some policies will tend to increase regional inequalities and some to diminish them. Among the latter are investment and land development programmes, and changes in taxation. These will benefit the poorer rural areas more than proportionately. On the other hand, higher grain prices will benefit the regions with a large marketable surplus and the input allocation policies will benefit regions with a high yield potential. It is safe to assume that these will be relatively prosperous regions. On balance, it is likely that regional inequalities will increase somewhat, especially in the short run when supply elasticities are low, but it is unlikely that, say, by the beginning of the next decade regional differentials will be noticeably different from what they are today. If this turns out to be the case, it would represent an impressive achievement in comparison with non-socialist developing economies, although in the context of Chinese socialism, it could legitimately be viewed with disappointment.

---

20 Report in *People's Daily*, 11 September 1980; SWB, FE/6532/C/4; 25 September 1980.

eight

Labour Absorption and Population Growth

The balance between the supply and demand for labour in rural areas affects both the level of output and the distribution of income. The sectoral allocation of labour among agriculture, industry and capital construction influences the pace of expansion and the composition of output. In this chapter we focus on several issues concerned with the utilization of manpower in the countryside. We begin with the demand side of the equation, looking first at the absorption of labour in agricultural production and then at the use of labour in rural investment projects. Next, we turn to rural industrialization and the role of manufacturing enterprises in providing employment and promoting rural development more generally. Finally, we look at the supply side and examine the new policies designed to reduce the rate of growth of the population.

The Absorption of Labour in Agriculture

One of the reasons why China was so successful in raising the standard of living and improving the distribution of income in rural areas is that she was able to provide ample employment for the labour force.[1] Some of this employment was generated in the state sector, in county factories and rural works programmes, but most of it was in the communes and it is on this that we will focus.

There are two separate aspects to rural employment. First, the provision of employment is a device for improving the degree of equality. Thus even when the entire labour force could not be used productively, and even in regions where there was considerable excess labour, full employment prevailed in the sense

---

1 The best study of this topic is Thomas G. Rawski, *Economic Growth and Employment in China*, Oxford University Press, 1979, Chapter Four.

that all ablebodied adults had the right, indeed the duty, to work on the collective. This entitled them to a regular share of the collective's income. Second, and equally important, is the role of employment in promoting growth and development. In China labour has been a major source of collective wealth and a highly adaptable agent of production.

The process generating employment within the commune reflects a continuous interplay between factors which enhance the demand for labour and those which release labour for other activities. This interplay is not a random or chance one, but is carefully mediated through commune level policies and underlines the remarkable developmental potential of the commune as an economic organization.

The origin of the process lies in the massive infrastructural and farm capital construction projects undertaken both at the local and the commune levels. These projects, relying heavily on large inputs of labour, were undertaken everywhere on a vast scale and they transformed the countryside. Examples include irrigation, drainage and flood control works; reclamation, terracing and levelling of arable land; afforestation and orchard planting; field consolidation and regularisation; construction of roads, bridges, schools and clinics. In recent years, about 30 per cent of the entire rural labour force has been involved in China's winter works campaigns and perhaps 20 per cent of the time of the rural labour force has been devoted to construction activities. When these programmes were first launched, rural labour was heavily underemployed, at least in a seasonal sense, and hence the opportunity cost of labour was minimal, especially given the distribution rules of the commune. It was therefore possible to undertake projects which on the surface might have appeared to be "uneconomic" if a shadow wage rate equal to the average income per worker had been used. Because in most areas labour was in short supply during the peak agricultural seasons, capital construction usually was undertaken during the off-peak periods. In this way the commune was able to internalize a wide range of external economies and undertake productive investments which were impossible to organize in pre-liberation rural China.

Employment was created by using labour to undertake investment and this, in turn, created the conditions for further employment. Thanks to the rapid expansion of the irrigated area, there was a considerable rise in the multiple cropping index. The percentage of cultivated area irrigated rose from 19.7 in 1952 to 44.9 in 1977, while the multiple cropping index rose over the same period from 1.31 to 1.58. Simultaneously, there was a change in the cropping pattern away from grains and in favour of labour intensive crops. Wheat, maize and rice — which in 1929 – 33 required, respectively, about 64, 57 and 203 mandays per hectare — gradually gave way to crops such as cotton, sugar, tobacco and tea — which required, respectively, about 131, 168, 218 and 312 man-days per hectare.

But while the number of harvests per hectare of land increased, there was no significant increase in the area cultivated. Instead, agriculture became more labour intensive. Cropping practices changed and in particular, much greater use was made of organic fertilizers, i.e., human and animal manure (especially pig manure), plant wastes and compost, ash, silt-bearing mud, etc. By 1971, about 156.1 kg. of organic fertilizer was applied to each cultivated hectare on average. This was 45.5 kg./ha. more than had been applied in 1957. At the same time, the use of chemical fertilizers increased very rapidly, from 3.4 kg./ha. in 1957 to 38.8 in 1971. Between 1952 and 1977, the use of all fertilizers (in nutrient terms) increased on average by 4.4 per cent a year.

Thomas Rawski estimates that during the period 1957 – 74 labour intensive agriculture grew 3.5 per cent a year whereas the output of grains increased only 2.1 per cent a year.[2] This change in the composition of output clearly helped to generate more employment for the agricultural labour force. Between 1957 and 1975 it is estimated that nearly 100 million new workers were able to obtain employment in the agricultural sector. In addition, the number of days worked per labourer increased from 175 – 190 days a year in the late 1950s to 272 – 284 days in 1975. In other words, the employed labour force increased by more than 40 per cent while the number of workdays per worker increased by more than 50 per cent. Today China enjoys virtually full employment in rural areas.

Far from having surplus labour, the rural areas of China are now characterized by a shortage of labour throughout most of the year. The shortage of labour does not imply that labour is highly productive, however. On the contrary, the enormous increase in labour absorption in rural areas has been achieved at the cost of a decline in the productivity of labour on the margin. That is, the number of days worked per worker has risen and this is associated with an increase of gross output per man-year and of income per household. But the marginal product of labour, output per man-day and the value of a work point have fallen.

The initial labour surplus is thus converted into a labour shortage. A fuller agricultural crop calendar leaves less time for farm capital construction and other infrastructural and residential projects. At the same time, the increased intensity of cultivation makes it both necessary and possible for the commune to engage in industrial production in support of agriculture. This, however, places a further demand on the agricultural labour force and provides a strong incentive to the commune to adopt active policies for farm mechanization in order to release labour for other uses. Not all mechanization, of course, is labour-displacing. Many forms of mechanization also are land-augmenting, e.g. investments which permit an extension of the area sown, or which raise crop yields through more timely land preparation and cultivation, or which reduce losses through speeding up harvesting operations.

The amount of investment in farm machinery in China has increased at a very rapid rate. In 1952 there were 2,000 tractor units of 15 horsepower. By 1977 the number had increased to 1.3 million. Similarly, between 1952 and 1977

2 *Ibid.*, Table 4 – 7, p. 107.

powered irrigation equipment increased from 183,000 horsepower to 66.5 million horsepower.[3] Farm machinery as a whole increased 23 per cent a year during this period.[4] Total farm capital (machinery plus livestock) rose by more than 150 per cent.[5] Despite this, value added per worker in agriculture declined from 218.3 yuan in 1952 to 199.7 yuan in 1977, a fall of 8.5 per cent.[6] Total factor productivity declined even more, namely, by 15 – 19 per cent.[7]

This, then, is the great irony of China's rural development. The country has been remarkably successful in mobilizing its labour force and providing employment for the rural population. But this success has been achieved at the expense of a fall in the marginal product of labour and in total factor productivity. The problem that must be solved now that full employment in the countryside has been attained is how to raise productivity while continuing to absorb the additions to the labour force. More investment within agriculture is part of the answer, as is an improved allocation of resources. Measures must also be taken to reduce the rate of growth of the population and labour force. But these alone will not suffice. The longer term answer must be found in the industrialization of the commune.

Indeed, increasing the labour absorptive capacity of commune industries is likely to become essential for further development. The scope for farm capital construction programmes is not unlimited; in fact, the more advanced communes in the developed regions probably have achieved about all that can be done in this area. A reduction in farm capital construction programmes is likely to release large amounts of seasonal labour, and it is unlikely that all of these labourers will be able to return to full time employment within an agricultural sector which has undergone a significant degree of mechanization. Moreover, one of the purposes of mechanization was to free the peasants from the drudgery of manual labour in the fields. This cannot now be reversed. It follows, then, that industries inside the commune represent a major potential labour receiving sector. Ideally, the pace of mechanization and the rate of expansion of industrial employment should be synchronized so as to achieve a continuous transformation of the commune's economy while maintaining full employment of the labour force. In practice, most communes are moving in the right direction, although not always as smoothly as might be desired. Especially in areas surrounding the great cities, the communes are in the process of making this last transition, one which transforms the rural people's commune from a predominantly agricultural economic organization into an industrial one.

Rural Industries

The fortunes of the rural industrial sector have fluctuated with major

3   Anthony M. Tang and Bruce Stone, *Food Production in the People's Republic of China*, IFPRI Research Report No. 15, May 1980, Table 18, p. 65.
4   *Ibid.*, p. 37
5   *Ibid.*, Table 4, p. 27.
6   *Ibid.*, Table 5, p. 28. The values are in 1952 yuan.
7   *Ibid.*

shifts in broad development strategy. Underneath these fluctuations, however, there has been considerable continuity and widespread agreement about the importance of the role performed by rural industries in agricultural modernization.[8] From their inception, commune industries have been expected to serve agricultural needs through the provision of intermediate inputs (e.g., fertilizers), small items of equipment (e.g. handtools) and a farm machinery workshop which services and repairs the larger farm machines. Additionally, commune enterprises provide support for the infrastructural activities within the commune through the provision of construction materials such as cement, bricks and wood. Furthermore, production within the commune of a range of consumption goods enables commune industries to raise the level of living of the peasantry and increase their incentives. Increasingly, however, commune level industries have entered production activities which are not connected directly to agriculture in the commune but which are linked instead to the urban industrial sector through a variety of sub-contracting arrangements. This bifurcation of the commune industrial sector in no way undermines its contributions to agricultural modernization. Indeed, industrial diversification strengthens the brigades and the commune, increases their financial resources and thereby augments their ability to assist in the fulfillment of the growth and distributional objectives of the collective institution.

We have noted already how the three-level ownership structure of the commune can be a powerful agent promoting capital accumulation and development. The thrust of this engine for growth comes from expansion of the industrial activities of the commune, and this expansion, in turn, leads to a steady increase in the importance of the two higher levels in the process of income generation. We have also remarked on the considerable potential of the commune organization for redistributing income and resources directly or indirectly towards the more disadvantaged units within the commune. The strength with which the redistributive mechanisms are brought into play depends, of course, in the first instance on the distributional policies of the commune leadership. More fundamental, however, is the size, composition and profitability of the brigade and commune level enterprises and particularly the extent of development of the commune's industrial sector.

Once one moves away from the locality, however, it is possible that the geographical pattern of development of the rural industrial sector aggravates regional income inequalities. There is, in fact, a very uneven regional pattern of location of commune industries. On average, there are about two brigade or commune level enterprises for each brigade or commune in China. Over 90 per cent of the communes and 80 per cent of the brigades have established some kind of enterprise. On average, income deriving from such enterprises accounts for approximately one-third of the total income of the three-level economy of the

---

8 See Jon Sigurdson, *Rural Industrialization in China*, Harvard University Press, 1977; Dwight Perkins *et al.*, *Rural Small-Scale Industry in the People's Republic of China*, University of California Press, 1977; Carl Riskin, "Small Industry and the Chinese Model of Development", *China Quarterly*, No. 46, 1971.

people's communes. However, these averages hide sharp regional differences: the percentage is 12 for Inner Mongolia, 16 for Xinjiang, 24.3 for Jiangxi, but as high as 65, 62, 57 and 43 for Shanghai, Suzhou and Beijing Municipalities and Hunan Province, respectively.

Such a wide variation was readily observable in the course of our field trip. Consider first Wu Gong Brigade in Hebei Province. Only 105 workers out of a total labour force of 1,197 are engaged in industry and sideline activities. They are employed in five establishments: 64 making rope from flax, 24 making string from paper, 6 each in a plastics and rubber workshop and 5 in a machine shop. More typical, perhaps, is Xin Tang Brigade of Tang Tang People's Commune which has only a small brick making enterprise and a repair workshop.

At the other extreme is Cheng Dong People's Commune in the Shanghai Municipality. Here nearly 47 per cent of the total income of the commune was produced in commune level enterprises in 1978. The major commune owned enterprises and the number of employees is as follows:

agricultural machinery repair workshop	171
towel manufacturing	350
plastics workshop	128
bamboo-ware workshop	93
manufacture of parts for lightbulbs	650
manufacture of spokes for bicycles	155
manufacture of lemon extract for export	102
construction team	400
waterway transportation team	153
tractor station	57

Cheng Dong, clearly, is a highly industrialized rural commune. Out of a total labour force of about 16,000, roughly 12 per cent, or 2,259 workers were engaged in commune level enterprises alone. In addition, there were another 2,457 workers engaged in brigade level industrial enterprises and 1,383 workers in brigade level sideline enterprises.

Thus, rural industries tend to be concentrated in the more industrialized regions such as the Shanghai and Beijing Municipalities, in rich agricultural zones enjoying high profits from the sale of above quota grain, and in areas blessed with mineral deposits or hydroelectric resources. Within local industry, the county's state-owned factories are more important than the commune's collectively owned enterprises. Looking at Chinese industry as a whole, rural industry in the counties and communes accounts for about a third of all industrial employment and 10 – 15 per cent of industrial output.[9] These proportions, although perhaps modest, are much higher today than they were in 1949. Furthermore, the recent shift in emphasis from heavy to light industry is likely to encourage rural industrialization even more. In fact it is probable that employ-

9   Thomas G. Rawski, *op. cit.*, p. 65.

ment and output of rural industries will remain one of the fastest growing sectors of the entire economy.

The widening impact on regional inequalities notwithstanding, rural industry makes an enormous contribution to the achievement of the growth and intra-regional distributional goals. This in itself constitutes a sufficient justification for the continuing, indeed increased, emphasis placed on the rural industrial sector. However, rural industry, especially commune industry contributes to national and local economic development in a great many other ways as well. Let us list these in a summary fashion and at the same time explain the role of the rural industrial sector in the Chinese context.[10]

1. First, there is the inadequacy of the Chinese transport network, especially in the rural areas. Transportation is unreliable, circuitous and expensive. This is especially true of the transport of some bulky products such as cement and bricks. In Lin County, it is reported that the cost of transporting coal 25 miles raised its price from 20 yuan to 30 yuan per ton.[11] Local industry helps to economize on transport.

2. Next, there is the problem of the planned allocation of producer goods to commune and brigade level enterprises. This can be a very time consuming and disrupting process to the industries concerned. Where the items involved are not very sophisticated, it may make sense in the longer run to create a capacity for production at the local level. This argument applies particularly to county rather than to commune and brigade level enterprises.

3. Commune industries are time-saving in at least three ways: they benefit from short gestation lags in construction; the down-time for their machines normally is shorter than in urban manufacturing establishments; and since they are based on local resources, production is less likely to be delayed because of supply bottlenecks.

4. Brigade and commune level industries rely heavily on local resources which have a low or zero opportunity cost for the modern sector. Many local resources therefore would remain unutilized if these industries did not exist.

5. Local rural industries have the advantage often of being labour intensive and hence of being able to absorb a significant proportion of the rural population in industrial activities. This not only generates incomes, it also creates other dynamic advantages such as the formation of skills. Commune industries contribute enormously to "learning-by-doing" and thereby pave the way subsequently for more sophisticated technology. This role of commune industry is increasingly evident, particularly in the more industrialized provinces.

6. Since commune and brigade level enterprises cater to local users, they have the advantage of being close to their market and being able to obtain information quickly on the performance of their products and on the precise nature of the demand for them. In some cases this is important for consumer

10 See also Dwight Perkins *et al.*, *op. cit.*, pp. 1 – 10.
11 *Ibid.*

goods, but it is even more important for some types of agricultural machines, e.g., in enabling the producer to adapt them better to the requirements of local cultivation. Proximity is not sufficient to ensure that rapid adaptation occurs, but it helps.

7. Commune industries also help to reduce inter-sectoral and inter-class income inequalities at the local level. It is not just the industrial workers of the commune or brigade enterprises who gain; the entire population of the brigade and commune gains. This is especially true when all or part of the wages are paid to the team from which a worker comes rather than directly to the worker. The wage payment system in the rural industrial sector evidently can be a very important instrument for achieving greater equality.

8. Socially, the industrial workers of local enterprises are not very different from the peasants from whose ranks they are drawn by their team or brigade leaders. They live in their teams and brigades and consequently their social, cultural and political lives are shared with the agricultural workers. In addition to the social advantages, this has an economic advantage as well in that the factory in the commune does not have to provide separate housing facilities for its workers or provide higher wages to enable workers to cover the cost of transport from home to factory.

9. This point can be taken further. Industrial development within the commune structure reduces the pressure for rural-urban migration and prevents the engorgement of cities that has caused so many difficulties in most non-socialist developing economies. As was stated in one recent report on China, "In fact, rural industries will often be the base from which new urban centres will arise. As rural small industries gradually expand in scale and number they will not be moved into existing urban centres. To the contrary, urbanization will be brought to them."[12]

Population Policies

Population policy in rural China recently has changed. At least until the middle of 1979 the norm in the countryside was two children, despite the fact that in the urban areas the one-child family increasingly was being advocated. Today, however, in the rural areas, too, incentives are being introduced to encourage couples to restrict the size of their family to three persons, i.e., the parents plus one child. The adoption of the norm of the one-child family constitutes a drastic social measure. This is apparent from the fact that at present there are, on average, 2.2 children per married couple in China.

The family planning programme can be visualized as a stool with three legs. First, there is the policy of late marriage. The minimum age for marriage in rural areas is 25 years for males and 23 for females. In the cities, the minimum age is slightly higher, namely, 26 and 24 years for males and females respectively. These limits were set in 1964 and have not been altered since then.

12 *Ibid.*, p. 255.

Second, the educational and propaganda systems are used to encourage married couples to delay pregnancy as long as possible. There are no financial rewards for delaying giving birth to a first child nor penalties for not delaying. Compliance is voluntary, although in small rural communities the attitudes of one's neighbours probably do have some effect on one's behaviour.

Third, there is the new element of providing material incentives to couples to have one child only. Contraceptives are supplied free of charge and are very widely used; sterilizations also are free and frequent, and in general mostly involve women. Abortions, too, are free of charge and in Chang Ching People's Commune, a rural commune in Suzhou Municipality in Jiangsu Province, women who have abortions within four months of conception are given 15 days of work points. Similar practices are common in other rural communes as well.

There are a series of recurrent economic benefits in Chang Ching Commune which together constitute a powerful inducement to limit the number of children to one per couple. A family with only one child receives an income supplement of 40 yuan a year from the commune's public welfare fund until the child is 14 years old. If the couple has a second child, however, the supplement not only is stopped but the couple is required to repay the accumulated sum of benefits previously received. Similarly, creche facilities in the commune are free for the first child, but couples have to pay about seven yuan a year for a second child. Again, one-child parents are given priority when allocating jobs in brigade and commune run enterprises; however, the job is lost should the couple have a second child. Since such jobs are worth about 50 yuan a year more than jobs at the level of the production team, a policy of linking employment allocations to family size could provide strong incentives to comply with the one child norm.

These incentives are further reinforced by giving an only child preference in brigade and commune run enterprises at age 16 when he or she joins the labour force. In addition, on the birth of a first child the family is allotted not one share of a private plot but two shares. This bonus for not having a second child is worth 0.07 mou in Chang Ching, or about 25 yuan a year in terms of income. This second share of a private plot is withdrawn if a couple has a second child. Finally, land is allocated for house construction by the production team in such a way as to encourage the one child family. It is customary in the area for enough land to be allocated to build two standard rooms per child. The one-child couple, however, is given enough land for four rooms. However, if the couple later has a second child, the extra land is taken away from the area devoted to their private plot. This deduction, moreover, is additional to the loss of the bonus of 0.07 mou just mentioned. The deduction of housing area alone is equivalent to about one-half of a private plot or, say, 12 – 15 yuan per year.

A rough calculation shows that compared with a couple that has a second child, the one-child family can increase its total household collective income by a quarter or a third. Evidently, this is a very strong incentive to conform to the norm. We do not pretend that this system of incentives is universal in the rural areas. But what is happening in Chang Ching probably indicates which way the wind is blowing. Certainly the Chinese are determined to reduce further the rate of demographic increase. The official objective is to lower it to one per cent per annum from the present rate of about 1.5 or 1.4 per cent.

This will not be an easy objective to achieve. There is a danger that in some localities over-zealous cadres will resort to coercion and in others the penalties for exceeding the norm of one child may be so severe as to be inhumane. There can be no doubt, however, that the broad objective of reducing fertility rates substantially is correct and perhaps even vital to increasing prosperity for the thousand million people who inhabit the country.

A sharp reduction of the rate of population increase through lower birth rates has several long term social and economic effects. In noting these, however, it is best to bear in mind that the new population control policies are likely to vary considerably from one region to another with regard to both the vigour with which the policies are implemented and the response of the masses to them. On the whole, it is likely that birth control measures will be more effectively implemented in the already densely populated rich regions of the country. This raises the question, therefore, of the likely impact of the new population policies on regional inequalities.

A sharp reduction of birth rates in rich regions would have the effect of raising the rate of growth of per capita income and of total output. Otherwise necessary recurrent expenditure on hospitals, schools, food and clothing, etc., would be unnecessary and these resources would become available, at least potentially, for productive investment. This would increase the rate of growth of output. In addition, the size of the population would be increasing at a slower pace. Therefore, the income gap between the poor regions with higher population growth rates and the rich regions would tend to widen. Of course, the age structure would be affected in the rich regions, but the labour force of the rich regions would nevertheless continue to increase for 50 years. It is unlikely, therefore, that the short to medium term beneficial growth impact in these regions would be eroded by any labour shortage in the longer term.

This deduction of widening inequalities between rich and poor regions is based on an assumption that the strength of application (and acceptance) of the new policies will turn out to be directly related to the current level of population pressure. It could be argued, however, that they will be related directly to the level of poverty itself. That is, poor regions have a greater need to restrain demographic increase and this will constitute a powerful incentive to do so. This seems a bit unlikely, but if it turns out to be the case, then population policies may not in practice have much effect either way on regional disparities.

nine

Rural Development Policy: Continuity and Change

Throughout this book we have pointed out the continuity in Chinese economic policy, its evolutionary nature and the underlying trends in growth and income distribution that stem from the institutional structure that was created in the 1950s. There is, however, another perspective that can be adopted, one that stresses discontinuities and radical reversals of policy. Phrases such as the Great Leap Forward, the Cultural Revolution and the Overthrow of the Gang of Four are evocative of the turbulence that has characterized the politics and economics of the country from time to time.

It can be argued, however, that both perspectives are correct, that is, that the turbulence has been concentrated in urban areas whereas the rural areas with which we are concerned have experienced fewer and less dramatic changes of course. Perhaps agriculture is inherently less amenable to frequent and radical alterations in direction because of the nature of the production process; or perhaps the political dangers that would result from a reduction in the availability of food predispose governments to be cautious when contemplating change in the countryside. Whatever the explanation, it seems clear to us that contemporary China is in large part a product of an agrarian revolution, but once the basic aims of the revolution had been achieved, the source of further change shifted from agriculture to the urban centres.

We try to show below that the rural development policies of the Gang of Four were not so different from those they attempted to supersede. Similarly, the new policies introduced in the second half of the 1970s can be regarded as marginal adjustments to earlier policies. On the other hand, this may be too sanguine a view. There must come a point at which the cumulative effects of a series of seemingly marginal adjustments transform the system into something else: quantitative change becomes qualitative change. We do not say that this has happened in rural China, or even that it is about to happen, but in the final paragraphs of the chapter we indicate that it might happen.

An Assessment of the Rural Economics of the "Gang of Four"

Recent changes in policies for rural development must be seen in the context of the attack on the views of the "Gang of Four" which began in October 1976. The general criticism of the "Gang of Four" is that they placed excessive emphasis on the "class struggle" to the relative neglect of the "struggle for production". That is, the followers of the "Gang of Four" are accused of giving too high a priority to the reduction of inequality.

The argument, of course, insofar as it is about economics, is about national priorities and not just about priorities for rural development. Hence one cannot evaluate the debate by referring only to evidence from the rural areas. Nevertheless, the evidence from the countryside is highly relevant since 81 per cent of the Chinese still live there. This evidence indicates, first, that the degree of equality in rural China is remarkably high by the standards of the Chinese past and of the other large Third World countries. Second, it appears that there are endogenous forces within the commune system which, at the local level, gradually are reducing inequality further. Third, this reduction in inequality has been accompanied, as we have seen, by a rate of growth of foodgrains, total agricultural production and total rural output (agricultural plus non-agricultural) that is clearly in excess of the rate of growth of the population. This does not prove that production could not have grown even faster if less egalitarian policies had been followed, but it does show that it is possible to achieve simultaneously a reduction in inequality and an increase in output per head.

The general criticism against the "Gang of Four" is supplemented by five additional charges. The first of these is the charge of "commandism". By "commandism" is meant a preference in favour of planning from the top down, a tendency toward dictatorial methods of management, a denial of local participation in decision making and a reliance on the political élite.

It is difficult to know how to assess this charge. Certainly there have been cases of labour from production teams being compelled to work on projects that benefit larger units, sometimes without pay, and of overzealous local officials arbitrarily increasing compulsory purchase quotas. The issue, however, seems wider than this. In any planned economy there is likely to be a conflict between the advantages of centralization and those of decentralization, between relying on planned prices or on quantitative controls and physical planning, and between the wish to extend the scope of the planned economy and the recognition of the uses of an unplanned sector. Moreover, the balance of advantage is likely to change from time to time in response to the development of the economy itself. Certainly the present administration in China has shifted the emphasis in favour of more local and enterprise autonomy, greater use of markets as an aid to planning and more tolerance of the private sector. All of these changes point toward less "commandism". At the same time, however, more emphasis has been placed on the role of managers, party officials, experts and technicians, and this equally could be interpreted as an élitist policy and hence as a form of "commandism". As regards participation, it is impossible not to be impressed by the participatory democracy which characterizes rural localities. The common people, ordinary peasants and workers, clearly do have a voice in making the decisions which affect their lives. But it is possible to argue that the degree of political, as against economic, participation has actually declined in the last couple of years. The long standing Poor and Poor-Middle Peasants Associations have been dissolved; Commune Revolutionary Committees have been relabelled Management Committees, reflecting the shift of emphasis in their role; Democracy Wall and the display of large character posters have been terminated; workers' political control over their enterprises has been curtailed; and the criticism of the "Gang of Four" by the masses appears no more or no less orchestrated than was the anti-Deng campaign earlier. No doubt the "Gang" and its followers can be charged with authoritarianism and arbitrariness in very many cases; it is too early to say, however, that the present regime in China will behave noticeably differently.

A second charge against the "Gang of Four" is that they placed excessive emphasis on capital accumulation and that this occurred at the expense of the consumption of the peasantry. In fact, the rate of investment in China has been quite high and rising for many years, viz., about 25 to 33 per cent of gross domestic product. Priority has been placed on the development of heavy industry and on relatively capital intensive techniques of production. Industrial output has increased more than 10 per cent a year on average for the last 30 years, almost all of it financed from internal sources under a policy of self-reliance.

Wages in state industry are substantially higher than the income of the peasantry. As a result, "the urban-rural incomes differential is something on the order of 2:1 (whether considered on a per capita or per labourer basis)."[1] Real wages in industry, however, remained almost constant for twenty years between 1957 and 1977. In late 1977 almost half the industrial labour force, notably the lower paid workers, received a modest increase in wages.

The present government has modified these policies in several ways. Less emphasis is placed on heavy industry and a higher priority has been given to investment in light industry and in agriculture. The overall rate of growth of the economy is to be accelerated under a "modernization" programme, while the living standards of the "masses", i.e. the peasantry, are to be raised quickly. Evidently these two objectives are potentially in conflict.

"Modernization" of the economy and a faster rate of growth requires more investment and consequently less consumption. Raising living standards quickly implies a higher proportion of national income being devoted to consumption and a lower proportion to investment. The leadership is attempting to

1 M.K. Whyte, "Inequality and Stratification in China", *China Quarterly*, No. 64, 1975, p. 687.

reconcile these conflicting implications by abandoning the policy of self-reliance and seeking capital abroad in the form of loans and joint ventures with private foreign corporations. It is possible that this strategy will work, but there is a great danger that foreign capital in effect will permit an increase in consumption while keeping the rates of accumulation and growth roughly constant. That is, there is a danger that the Chinese will end up borrowing abroad in order to increase consumption. It is doubtful that this would be in the long run interests of the peasantry. Alternatively, there is a danger that the Chinese will resist the temptation to borrow heavily abroad while maintaining a commitment to increasing current consumption. In this case investment will fall and with it the growth rate, unless the effectiveness of investment rises.

Third, the "Gang of Four" are charged with placing excessive emphasis on grain production with a consequent misallocation of land and a neglect of opportunities for regional specialization. Local self-sufficiency in grain certainly has been a feature of China's agricultural policy and direct consumption of foodgrains is among the highest in the world. Hence it is reasonable to expect that future plans will give relatively high priority to improving diets by increasing the production and consumption of items other than wheat and rice.[2] This will enable China to reallocate marginal land presently devoted to wheat and other grains to such things as pastures, forests, oil crops, pulses and sugar beets. The scope for such a reallocation should not be exaggerated, however.

The original justification for a policy of local self-sufficiency in grain was only partly ideological. Also important was the defence argument, namely, the need for the people to be able to continue to subsist and resist even if an invading army were to occupy large parts of China's territory. Finally, whatever the ideological and military arguments, the fact remains that the possibilities of rapidly changing agricultural specialization by region are severely limited by the poor transportation system and the resulting high cost of transport. No doubt opportunities for greater specialization do exist, and the government is right to want to take greater advantage of them, but a radical change in policy will not be possible until the inland transportation system improves considerably.

"Adventurism" is the fourth charge. This refers to an alleged tendency to rush prematurely into more advanced forms of socialist organization. Specifically, the "Gang of Four" are accused of exerting pressure on members of communes to raise the level of accounts from the teams to brigade or even commune level. The main advantage of raising the level of accounts from, say, the team to the brigade is that it ensures equal reward for equal work throughout the production brigade and not just throughout the team. That is, it ensures that the value of a work point becomes uniform throughout the brigade. The reason for this is that the value of a work point is determined by dividing a unit's (team or brigade or entire commune as the case may be) collective output by the total number of work points. Thus if output per man varies from one

---

2 Shigeru Ishikawa, "China's Food and Agriculture: A Turning Point", *Food Policy*, May 1977.

team to another, the value of a work point also will vary, as will income per man. By raising the level of accounts from the team to the brigade these variations will be averaged out and a greater degree of equality will be achieved.

There are only 60 out of some 53,000 communes in the entire country which keep their accounts at commune level, and these are mainly pastoral or fishing communes. In the province of Hebei about 12 per cent of the production brigades keep their accounts at brigade level. In the country as a whole the proportion is about 7 or 8 per cent. In other words, in the great majority of communes the level at which accounts are kept is the production team, the smallest unit of collective economic activity.

We were unable to find any evidence that the small minority of communes which kept accounts at brigade or commune levels did so as a result of political pressure from the "Gang of Four" and their followers. Be that as it may, the present government has reaffirmed the team as the basic accounting unit. The level of accounts normally would not be raised to a higher level unless

(a) the leaders are capable of managing larger sized units,

(b) the differences in average incomes among teams already are fairly narrow,

(c) the higher unit already accounts for over half of collective output and

(d) there is mass, voluntary support for doing so.

That is, a change in the level of accounts is supposed to reflect changes in economic circumstances ("objective conditions") and political preferences ("subjective conditions"); it is not intended to be used as a general policy instrument to bring about a more efficient use of resources and a more equal distribution of income. In our opinion, this is a pity.

The final charge is "ultra-egalitarianism". The "Gang of Four" are accused of advocating a payment system which emphasizes payment according to need (a communist principle) at the expense of work incentives and payment according to work (a socialist principle). The debate revolves around the proportion of collective distributed grain that should be allocated on a per capita basis rather than on a work point basis.

The ultra-egalitarians favoured distributing 90 per cent of the grain on an equal per capita basis, leaving only 10 per cent to be distributed according to the number of work points earned. The present government regards this policy as damaging to incentives and wants the basic grain ration to be reduced from 90 to 70 per cent;[3] the amount distributed according to work would therefore rise from 10 to 30 per cent. The debate clearly is important in the Chinese context and raises ideological issues as well as technical questions about the responsiveness of effort and output to changes in the payments system. Seen from the perspective of the capitalist countries, however, the remarkable thing is that the rural economy in China seems to have functioned well with a payments system in which most of the grain (be it 70 or 90 per cent) was distributed according to

3 There are considerable variations in this percentage across regions, and across communes within the same region.

need. Those who believe that large wage and income differentials are essential for efficient production can learn much from the Chinese experience.

The impression derived from our field observations in June 1979 was that the new policies for rural development represented essentially attempts at fine tuning: a bit more local autonomy in decision making, a bit more regional specialization, a bit more freedom for private economic activities, a bit more reliance on material incentives and fewer attempts to achieve more advanced forms of socialism. These appeared to be modest changes and most of them probably were desirable as well. Certainly at that time, the changes in rural areas were much less dramatic than the new policies introduced in industry and foreign commerce.

Piecemeal Reforms versus Systemic Change

The opportunity to work in the field, to conduct research at the local level, enabled us to obtain many illuminating insights. This method of research, however, also has its limitations and raises important issues about how to interpret field data. Specifically, what we obtained on our field trip was a still picture of a thin slice of rural China. Even this still picture was partially blurred because the subject itself was in motion. We felt then that the motion was insignificant and could not in itself be regarded as evidence of a major change in policy, much less of a systemic change. Yet it is possible that such a conclusion, warranted as it might have been on our limited evidence, would nevertheless be misleading given the benefit of hindsight. In the course of a second field trip in rural China, one of us obtained a second snapshot of our moving subject.[4] Using this as well as reports which subsequently have appeared in the Chinese media, it is possible to construct an animated, albeit disjointed view of the direction and pace of change in rural China.

There is one problem, however, that confronts anyone interested in interpreting events in contemporary China, as opposed merely to describing them. This concerns the extent to which piecemeal, marginal policy changes can be viewed in isolation rather than as related pieces in a pattern of systemic or fundamental change. Thus, in our field work, relatively small changes were observed in several aspects of rural economic policy, but precisely because of the marginality of each change, the question of whether these added up to a systemic change was never seriously examined.

Many of the marginal changes of 1979, however, have since grown into more significant ones. Consider two illustrations. During the field trip we were told by high officials and peasants alike that Dazhai was still a model to be emulated, although one should take local variations into account as well as the need to provide work incentives. A year later the situation was rather different: Dazhai work methods were no longer thought to be suitable, although the

---

4 Ashwani Saith studied the operation of new policies in communes in Suzhou Municipality in June 1980.

general approach of this model brigade was still accepted. Six months later, the Dazhai model not only was repudiated, it was utterly discredited.

Again, during our field trip we enquired into work groups. We were interested in knowing whether they were common and whether they were serving also as units of account. We were told that they did exist — indeed we saw some ourselves — but both officials and peasants insisted that work groups would not become a fourth level below the level of the production team. A year later, officials said there was a general policy to encourage work groups but that these groups were essentially managerial and organization devices; there was no intention of altering income-accounting procedures. Six months later, in several parts of China, work groups had become in practice accounting units, and in some areas the accounting level has been reduced in effect to individual households.

These examples can be multiplied. The systematic relaxation of policies controlling the private sector is a third illustration of an initially small change growing into a significant one. Perhaps these illustrations should be regarded as random happenings, or as a consequence of local officials taking policies beyond the limits intended by the central authorities, or as a glimpse of a pendulum that soon will begin to swing in the opposite direction. Viewed together, however, these illustrations also raise the real possibility that what we regarded in June 1979 as independent and marginal policy adjustments were in fact the initial, tentative applications of a new and systematic policy for fundamental institutional change in the Chinese countryside.

Index

164

Five guarantees, 130-1
Fo Gang County, 6, 17, 23, 24-5, 36,
128

- G -

Gang of Four, 1, 4, 12, 157-62
Grain pricing, 3-4, 7, 140, 143
Great Leap Forward, 123, 133, 143,
157
Growth, 4, 11, 55, 93-5, 121-2, 126-8,
159-60
  and income distribution, 55-8,
  95-115
Guangdong Province, 6, 15, 17, 20,
23, 130, 141

- H -

Hay, Roger, 1
Hebei Province, 2-3, 4, 15, 17, 18-21,
55-6, 126, 128, 130, 150
Hinton, William, 123n
Huan Xiang, 1

- I -

Incentives, 2, 3, 125, 143
Income, distribution of, 1, 4, 10-11,
15-25, 121-2, 128-35
  among brigades, 27-41
  among communes, 21-5
  among households, 47-51,
  125-6, 130
  among teams, 41-7
Income inequality, 2, 11-2, 133, 135,
158
Industry, 12, 28, 64-5, 124, 127, 135,
137-8, 143, 145, 147, 148-52, 159
Institute of Agricultural Economics, 1
Institutional framework, 121-8
Investment, see capital accumulation
Irrigation, 2, 25, 44-5, 139, 146
Ishikawa, Shigeru, 160n

- J -

Jia Ding County, 4, 6, 17, 23, 55, 128
Jiangsu Province, 4, 136, 142

- L -

Lardy, Nicholas, 135n, 137

- M -

Marshall, Marsh, 1
Maxwell, Neville, 1, 131n
Medical care, 2, 124, 132

- N -

Nolan, Peter, 1

- P -

Participation, 159
Perkins, Dwight, 149n, 151n, 152n
Planning, 126-8, 158
Policies, 12, 56, 110, 115-8, 129-30,
157-63
  and intra-rural income
  distribution, 131-5
Population, growth of, 144, 154, 158
  policies, 12, 152-4
Prices, 2, 117-8, 136, 140, 144
Private sector, 2, 3, 6-7, 16-17, 49-51,
125-6, 131-2, 134, 141-2, 158, 163
Productivity, 11, 37-41, 63-64, 117,
133, 147-8

- Q -

Qie Ma People's Commune, 3, 17,
27-8, 33-4, 56, 129
Queen Elizabeth House, 1
Quotas, 3, 140, 143

- R -

Rath, N., 136n
Rawski, Thomas G., 145n, 147, 150n

THE AUTHORS

Keith Griffin is President of Magdalen College, Oxford and Director of the Contemporary China Centre. He was formerly Warden of Queen Elizabeth House and Director of the Institute of Commonwealth Studies at Oxford. He has served as an adviser and consultant to various governments, international agencies and academic institutions in Asia, Latin America and North Africa. He is the author of many articles and books including "The Political Economy of Agrarian Change", "International Inequality and National Poverty", "Land Concentration and Rural Poverty" and (with Jeffrey James) "The Transition to Egalitarian Development".

Ashwani Saith graduated and took a Master's degree while at St. Stephen's College, Delhi, and subsequently completed his doctorate at Trinity College, Cambridge. Prior to taking up his current post of Professor of Rural Economics at the Institute of Social Studies at The Hague, he was Research Fellow at Queen Elizabeth House, Oxford. He has published articles in various academic journals, and is currently engaged in completing two studies concerned separately with the processes of agrarian transformation in colonial and post-colonial India.